VB.NET IDE

CODE USING

ADO

Routines you can use over and over again

Richard Thomas Edwards

What is in store for you
Do you really want to keep writing code over and over again?

I think is was Albert Einstein who said the definition of being insane is to do the same thing over and over again expecting different results. Perhaps, not him although he seems to be one of many claiming such lines.

The point is, the reason why I am writing this e-book, you can write a single routine the correct way and never have to write it again.

And, yes, you can have different outcomes.

Simply change the connection string and or the SQL string and the view in its tidy design is there for you to blow your competition away with his non-labor cost and speed by which you were able to write the code effortlessly.

If it sounds to good to be true, I ask, how many times do you need to write the following?

```
Public Function Test_Connection_to_Database(ByVal cnstr As String) As string

    Dim cn as Adodb.Connection
    Try
        Cn.ConnectionString = cnstr
```

```
    Cn.Open()
    Return "Connection was Successful"
Catch ex as Exception
    Return "Connection failed for the following reason: " & ex.Message
End Try

End Function
```

Or this one:

```
Public Function Get_Tables_From_Access_Database(ByVal cnstr As String) As Datatable
    Dim cn As New System.Data.OleDb.OleDbConnection(cnstr)
    cn.Open()

    Dim dt As System.Data.DataTable = cn.GetSchema("Tables")

    Return dt
End Function
```

I think you're getting the point. There is no reason for common routines to be written by you or anyone else. It is simply a waste of time, effort and less idle time for you.

Take it from experience, you never know when someone is looking for a clutch program that you have already created – one that could take a day or longer to write from scratch – and have available that saves the day and makes everyone happy.

Including your new boss.

So, with that said, this book is about creating routines you put into a module, make two calls to that module and it produces visual results. The core building blocks looks like this:

```
Imports ADODB
Module Module1
```

```vb
Dim rs as new ADODB.Recordset

Public Sub Create_Recordset(ByVal cnstr as String, ByVal strQuery as String,
ByVal Tablename as String)

    'the code could be this

    Rs.ActiveConnection = cnstr
    Rs.CursorLocation = 3
    Rs.LockType = 3
    Rs.Source = strQuery
    Rs.Open()

    'or this:

    Rs.let_ActiveConnection(cnstr)
    Rs.CursorLocation = 3
    Rs.LockType = 3
    Rs.let_Source(strQuery)
    Rs.Open()


    'or this:

    Rs.ActiveConnection(cnstr)
    Rs.CursorLocation = 3
    Rs.LockType = 3
    Rs.Open(strQuery)

    'or what works for you. I'm just showing you what works for me.

End Sub
```

```vbnet
Public Sub populate_Datagridview_Using_A_Recordset(ByVal rs As Object, ByVal
Dg1 As DataGridView, ByVal Orientation As String)

    Dim x As Integer = 0
    Dim y As Integer = 0

    Select Case Orientation

        Case "Single Line Horizontal"

            For x = 0 To rs.Fields.Count - 1
                Dg1.Columns.Add(rs.Fields(x).Name, rs.Fields(x).Name)
            Next
            Dg1.Rows.Add()
            Rs.MoveFirst()
            For x = 0 To rs.Fields.Count - 1
                Try
                    Dg1.Rows(0).Cells(x).Value = rs.Fields(x).Value
                Catch ex As Exception
                    Dg1.Rows(0).Cells(x).Value = ""
                End Try
            Next

        Case "Multi Line Horizontal"

            For x = 0 To rs.Fields.Count - 1
                Dg1.Columns.Add(rs.Fields(x).Name, rs.Fields(x).Name)
            Next
            Rs.MoveFirst()
            Do While rs.EOF = False
                Dg1.Rows.Add()
                For x = 0 To rs.Fields.Count - 1
                    Try
                        Dg1.Rows(y).Cells(x).Value = rs.Fields(x).Value
                    Catch ex As Exception
                        Dg1.Rows(y).Cells(x).Value = ""
                    End Try
                Next
                y = y + 1
                rs.MoveNext()
            Loop

        Case "Single Line Vertical"

            Dg1.Columns.Add("Property Name", "Property Name")
            Dg1.Columns.Add("Property Value", "Property Value")
            For x = 0 To rs.Fields.Count - 1
                Dg1.Rows.Add()
                Dg1.Rows(x).Cells(0).Value = rs.Fields(x).Name
                Try
```

```vbnet
            Dg1.Rows(x).Cells(1).Value = rs.Fields(x).Value
          Catch ex As Exception
            Dg1.Rows(x).Cells(1).Value = ""
          End Try
        Next

      Case "Multi Line Vertical"

        Dg1.Columns.Add(" Property Name", "Property Name")

        For y = 0 To rs.RecordCount - 1
          Dg1.Columns.Add("Row" & y, "Row" & y)
        Next

        For x = 0 To rs.Fields.Count - 1
          Dg1.Rows.Add()
          Dg1.Rows(x).Cells(0).Value = rs.Fields(x).Name
          rs.MoveFirst()
          y = 0
          Do While rs.Eof = False
            Try
              Dg1.Rows(x).Cells(y + 1).Value = rs.Fields(x).Value
            Catch ex As Exception
              Dg1.Rows(x).Cells(y + 1).Value = ""
            End Try
            y = y + 1
            Rs.MoveNext()
          Loop
        Next

    End Select



  End Sub
```

For testing purposes, I created a form and placed on the form a Splitter Control, put 4 buttons on it and put the DataGridView1 control in the right panel. Under each button, I put the code below:

```vbnet
Private Sub Button1_Click(sender As System.Object, e As System.EventArgs)
Handles Button1.Click

  Dim cn As Object = CreateObject("ADODB.Connection")
```

```vb
    cn.ConnectionString = "Provider=Microsoft.Jet.OleDb.4.0;Data
Source=C:\Program Files (x86)\Microsoft Visual Studio\VB98\NWind.mdb"
    cn.Open("")

    Dim rs As Object = CreateObject("ADODB.Recordset")
    rs.ActiveConnection = cn
    rs.CursorLocation = 3
    rs.LockType = 3
    rs.Source = "Select * From Products"
    rs.Open()

    populate_Datagridview_Using_A_Recordset(rs, DataGridView1, "Single Line
Horizontal")

    End Sub

    Private Sub Button2_Click(sender As System.Object, e As System.EventArgs)
Handles Button2.Click

    Dim cn As Object = CreateObject("ADODB.Connection")
    cn.ConnectionString = "Provider=Microsoft.Jet.OleDb.4.0;Data
Source=C:\Program Files (x86)\Microsoft Visual Studio\VB98\NWind.mdb"
    cn.Open("")

    Dim rs As Object = CreateObject("ADODB.Recordset")
    rs.ActiveConnection = cn
    rs.CursorLocation = 3
    rs.LockType = 3
    rs.Source = "Select * From Products"
    rs.Open()

    populate_Datagridview_Using_A_Recordset(rs, DataGridView1, "Multi Line
Horizontal")

    End Sub

    Private Sub Button3_Click(sender As System.Object, e As System.EventArgs)
Handles Button3.Click

    Dim cn As Object = CreateObject("ADODB.Connection")
    cn.ConnectionString = "Provider=Microsoft.Jet.OleDb.4.0;Data
Source=C:\Program Files (x86)\Microsoft Visual Studio\VB98\NWind.mdb"
    cn.Open("")

    Dim rs As Object = CreateObject("ADODB.Recordset")
    rs.ActiveConnection = cn
    rs.CursorLocation = 3
    rs.LockType = 3
    rs.Source = "Select * From Products"
    rs.Open()
```

populate_Datagridview_Using_A_Recordset(rs, DataGridView1, "Single Line Vertical")

End Sub

Private Sub Button4_Click(sender As System.Object, e As System.EventArgs) Handles Button4.Click

```
Dim cn As Object = CreateObject("ADODB.Connection")
cn.ConnectionString = "Provider=Microsoft.Jet.OleDb.4.0;Data
Source=C:\Program Files (x86)\Microsoft Visual Studio\VB98\NWind.mdb"
cn.Open("")

Dim rs As Object = CreateObject("ADODB.Recordset")
rs.ActiveConnection = cn
rs.CursorLocation = 3
rs.LockType = 3
rs.Source = "Select * From Products"
rs.Open()
```

populate_Datagridview_Using_A_Recordset(rs, DataGridView1, "Multi Line Vertical")

End Sub

It looks like this:

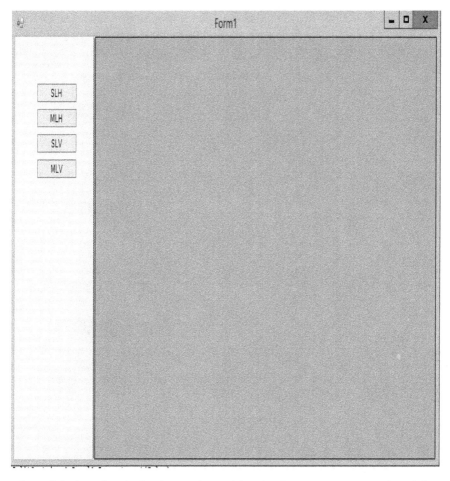

When clicked on the Single Line Horizontal (SLH). The test program produced this:

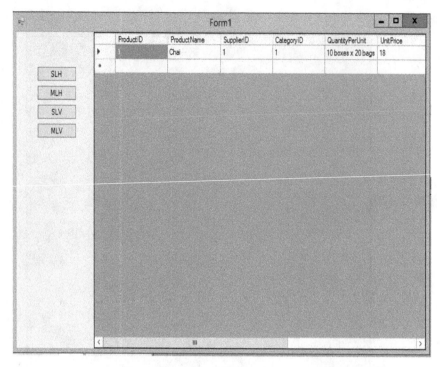

When I clicked on the Multi Line Horizontal, it returned this:

ProductID	ProductName	SupplierID	CategoryID	QuantityPerUnit	UnitPrice
1	Chai	1	1	10 boxes x 20 bags	18
2	Chang	1	1	24 - 12 oz bottles	19
3	Aniseed Syrup	1	2	12 - 550 ml bottles	10
4	Chef Anton's Caj...	2	2	48 - 6 oz jars	22
5	Chef Anton's Gu...	2	2	36 boxes	21.35
6	Grandma's Boyse...	3	2	12 - 8 oz jars	25
7	Uncle Bob's Orga...	3	7	12 - 1 lb pkgs.	30
8	Northwoods Cran...	3	2	12 - 12 oz jars	40
9	Mishi Kobe Niku	4	6	18 - 500 g pkgs.	97
10	Ikura	4	8	12 - 200 ml jars	31
11	Queso Cabrales	5	4	1 kg pkg.	21
12	Queso Mancheg...	5	4	10 - 500 g pkgs.	38
13	Konbu	6	8	2 kg box	6
14	Tofu	6	7	40 - 100 g pkgs.	23.25
15	Genen Shouyu	6	2	24 - 250 ml bottles	15.5
16	Pavlova	7	3	32 - 500 g boxes	17.45
17	Alice Mutton	7	6	20 - 1 kg tins	39
18	Carnarvon Tigers	7	8	16 kg pkg.	62.5
19	Teatime Chocolat...	8	3	10 boxes x 12 pie...	9.2
20	Sir Rodney's Mar...	8	3	30 gift boxes	81

When I clicked on the Single Line Vertical, it produced this:

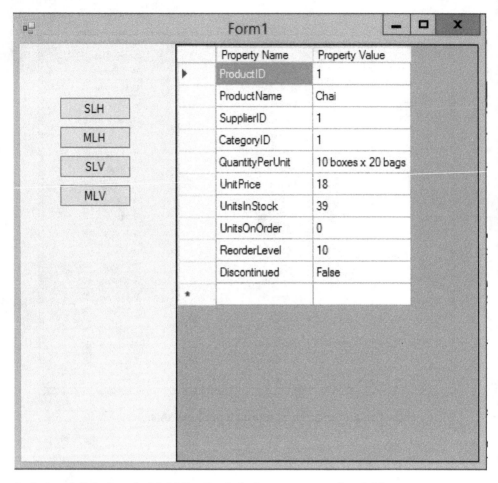

And when I clicked on the Multi line Vertical, the program produced this:

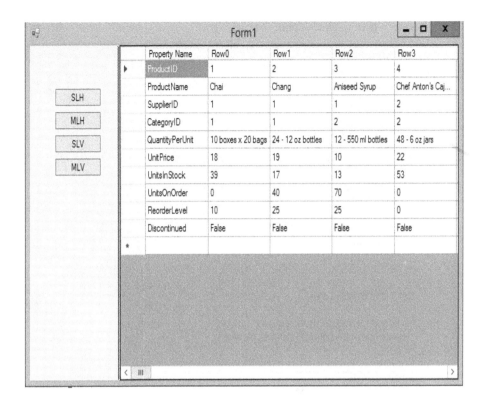

Property Name	Row0	Row1	Row2	Row3
ProductID	1	2	3	4
ProductName	Chai	Chang	Aniseed Syrup	Chef Anton's Caj...
SupplierID	1	1	1	2
CategoryID	1	1	2	2
QuantityPerUnit	10 boxes x 20 bags	24 - 12 oz bottles	12 - 550 ml bottles	48 - 6 oz jars
UnitPrice	18	19	10	22
UnitsInStock	39	17	13	53
UnitsOnOrder	0	40	70	0
ReorderLevel	10	25	25	0
Discontinued	False	False	False	False

But this is just the tip of the iceberg so to speak as we can also create the same exact views using the DataSet, DataTable and DataView:

```
Public Sub PopulateDataGridView_Using_A_Dataset(ByVal rs As Object, ByVal Dg1
As DataGridView, ByVal Orientation As String)


    Dim x As Integer = 0
    Dim y As Integer = 0

    Dim ds As New System.Data.DataSet
    Dim dt As System.Data.DataTable

    Select Case Orientation

        Case "Single Line Horizontal"

            dt = New System.Data.DataTable
```

```vbnet
        For x = 0 To rs.Fields.Count − 1

            dt.Columns.Add(rs.Fields(x).Name)

        Next

        rs.MoveFirst()
        Dim dr As System.Data.DataRow = dt.NewRow
        For x = 0 To rs.Fields.Count - 1
            Try
                dr.Item(rs.Fields(x).Name) = rs.Fields(x).Value
            Catch ex As Exception
                dr.Item(rs.Fields(x).Name) = ""
            End Try
        Next
        dt.Rows.Add(dr)
        ds.Tables.Add(dt)

    Case "Multi Line Horizontal"

        dt = New System.Data.DataTable

        For x = 0 To rs.Fields.Count - 1
            dt.Columns.Add(rs.Fields(x).Name)
        Next

        rs.MoveFirst()
        Do While rs.EOF = False
            Dim dr As System.Data.DataRow = dt.NewRow
            For x = 0 To rs.Fields.Count - 1
                Try
                    dr.Item(rs.Fields(x).Name) = rs.Fields(x).Value
                Catch ex As Exception
                    dr.Item(rs.Fields(x).Name) = ""
                End Try
            Next
            dt.Rows.Add(dr)
            rs.MoveNext()
        Loop

        ds.Tables.Add(dt)

    Case "Single Line Vertical"

        dt = New System.Data.DataTable

        dt.Columns.Add("Property Name")
        dt.Columns.Add("Property Value")

        For x = 0 To rs.Fields.Count - 1
```

```
            Dim dr As System.Data.DataRow = dt.NewRow()
            dr.Item("Property Name") = rs.Fields(x).Name
            Try
               dr.Item("Property Value") = rs.Fields(x).Value
            Catch ex As Exception
               dr.Item("Property Value") = ""
            End Try
            dt.Rows.Add(dr)
         Next

         ds.Tables.Add(dt)

      Case "Multi Line Vertical"

         dt = New System.Data.DataTable
         dt.Columns.Add("Property Name")

         For y = 0 To rs.RecordCount - 1
            dt.Columns.Add("Row" & y)
         Next

         For x = 0 To rs.Fields.Count - 1
            Dim dr As System.Data.DataRow = dt.NewRow
            dr.Item("Property Name") = rs.Fields(x).Name
            rs.MoveFirst()
            y = 0
            Do While rs.Eof = False
               Try
                  dr.Item("Row" & y) = rs.Fields(x).Value
               Catch ex As Exception
                  dr.Item("Row" & y) = ""
               End Try
               y = y + 1
               rs.MoveNext()
            Loop
            dt.Rows.Add(dr)
         Next

         ds.Tables.Add(dt)

   End Select

   Dg1.DataSource = ds.Tables(0)


End Sub
```

```vb
Public Sub PopulateDataGridView_Using_A_DataTable(ByVal rs As Object, ByVal
Dg1 As DataGridView, ByVal Orientation As String)


    Dim x As Integer = 0
    Dim y As Integer = 0


    Dim dt As System.Data.DataTable

    Select Case Orientation

        Case "Single Line Horizontal"

            dt = New System.Data.DataTable

            For x = 0 To rs.Fields.Count - 1
                dt.Columns.Add(rs.Fields(x).Name)
            Next

            rs.MoveFirst()
            Dim dr As System.Data.DataRow = dt.NewRow
            For x = 0 To rs.Fields.Count - 1
                Try
                    dr.Item(rs.Fields(x).Name) = rs.Fields(x).Value
                Catch ex As Exception
                    dr.Item(rs.Fields(x).Name) = ""
                End Try
            Next
            dt.Rows.Add(dr)

        Case "Multi Line Horizontal"

            dt = New System.Data.DataTable

            For x = 0 To rs.Fields.Count - 1
                dt.Columns.Add(rs.Fields(x).Name)
            Next

            rs.MoveFirst()
            Do While rs.EOF = False
                Dim dr As System.Data.DataRow = dt.NewRow
                For x = 0 To rs.Fields.Count - 1
                    Try
                        dr.Item(rs.Fields(x).Name) = rs.Fields(x).Value
                    Catch ex As Exception
                        dr.Item(rs.Fields(x).Name) = ""
                    End Try
                Next
                dt.Rows.Add(dr)
```

```vbnet
        rs.MoveNext()
    Loop


Case "Single Line Vertical"

    dt = New System.Data.DataTable

    dt.Columns.Add("Property Name")
    dt.Columns.Add("Property Value")

    For x = 0 To rs.Fields.Count - 1
        Dim dr As System.Data.DataRow = dt.NewRow()
        dr.Item("Property Name") = rs.Fields(x).Name
        Try
            dr.Item("Property Value") = rs.Fields(x).Value
        Catch ex As Exception
            dr.Item("Property Value") = ""
        End Try
        dt.Rows.Add(dr)
    Next


Case "Multi Line Vertical"

    dt = New System.Data.DataTable
    dt.Columns.Add("Property Name")

    For y = 0 To rs.RecordCount - 1
        dt.Columns.Add("Row" & y)
    Next

    For x = 0 To rs.Fields.Count - 1
        Dim dr As System.Data.DataRow = dt.NewRow
        dr.Item("Property Name") = rs.Fields(x).Name
        rs.MoveFirst()
        y = 0
        Do While rs.Eof = False
            Try
                dr.Item("Row" & y) = rs.Fields(x).Value
            Catch ex As Exception
                dr.Item("Row" & y) = ""
            End Try
            y = y + 1
            rs.MoveNext()
        Loop
        dt.Rows.Add(dr)
    Next
```

```vbnet
        End Select

        Dg1.DataSource = dt


    End Sub


    Public Sub PopulateDataGridView_Using_A_DataView(ByVal rs As Object, ByVal
Dg1 As DataGridView, ByVal Orientation As String)


        Dim x As Integer = 0
        Dim y As Integer = 0


        Dim dt As System.Data.DataTable = New System.Data.DataTable
        Dim dv As System.Data.DataView = dt.DefaultView


        Select Case Orientation

            Case "Single Line Horizontal"


                For x = 0 To rs.Fields.Count - 1
                    dv.Table.Columns.Add(rs.Fields(x).Name)
                Next

                rs.MoveFirst()
                Dim dr As System.Data.DataRow = dv.Table.NewRow
                For x = 0 To rs.Fields.Count - 1
                    Try
                        dr.Item(rs.Fields(x).Name) = rs.Fields(x).Value
                    Catch ex As Exception
                        dr.Item(rs.Fields(x).Name) = ""
                    End Try
                Next
                dv.Table.Rows.Add(dr)

            Case "Multi Line Horizontal"

                dt = New System.Data.DataTable

                For x = 0 To rs.Fields.Count - 1
                    dv.Table.Columns.Add(rs.Fields(x).Name)
                Next

                rs.MoveFirst()
```

```vbnet
   Do While rs.EOF = False
      Dim dr As System.Data.DataRow = dv.Table.NewRow
      For x = 0 To rs.Fields.Count - 1
         Try
            dr.Item(rs.Fields(x).Name) = rs.Fields(x).Value
         Catch ex As Exception
            dr.Item(rs.Fields(x).Name) = ""
         End Try
      Next
      dv.Table.Rows.Add(dr)
      rs.MoveNext()
   Loop


Case "Single Line Vertical"

   dt = New System.Data.DataTable

   dv.Table.Columns.Add("Property Name")
   dv.Table.Columns.Add("Property Value")

   For x = 0 To rs.Fields.Count - 1
      Dim dr As System.Data.DataRow = dv.Table.NewRow()
      dr.Item("Property Name") = rs.Fields(x).Name
      Try
         dr.Item("Property Value") = rs.Fields(x).Value
      Catch ex As Exception
         dr.Item("Property Value") = ""
      End Try
      dv.Table.Rows.Add(dr)
   Next


Case "Multi Line Vertical"

   dt = New System.Data.DataTable
   dv.Table.Columns.Add("Property Name")

   For y = 0 To rs.RecordCount - 1
      dv.Table.Columns.Add("Row" & y)
   Next

   For x = 0 To rs.Fields.Count - 1
      Dim dr As System.Data.DataRow = dv.Table.NewRow
      dr.Item("Property Name") = rs.Fields(x).Name
      rs.MoveFirst()
      y = 0
      Do While rs.Eof = False
         Try
            dr.Item("Row" & y) = rs.Fields(x).Value
```

```
        Catch ex As Exception
            dr.Item("Row" & y) = ""
        End Try
        y = y + 1
        rs.MoveNext()
    Loop
    dv.Table.Rows.Add(dr)
Next


End Select

Dg1.DataSource = dv

End Sub
```

A few questions which need to be answered. If we are using the DataGridView1's DataSource, why couldn't we simply use the OleDbDataAdapter and wire the DataSet, DataTable or DataView to the existing recordset?

The answer is, of course we could:

```
Dim ds as new System.Data.DataSet
Dim da as new System.Data.OleDb.OleDbDataAdapter
Da.Fill(ds, rs, "Products")

Dg1.DataSource = ds.Tables(0)
```

Or:

```
Dim dt as new System.Data.DataTable
Dim da as new System.Data.OleDb.OleDbDataAdapter
Da.Fill(dt, rs)

Dg1.DataSource = dt
```

Or:

```
Dim dt as new System.Data.DataTable
Dim da as new System.Data.OleDb.OleDbDataAdapter
Da.Fill(dt, rs)
Dim dv as System.Data.DataView = dt.DefaultView
Dg1.DataSource = dv
```

All of the above will work but the only view you would get from the above code would be how the Recordset is oriented and most tables are by default oriented with a horizontal view.

The other question is: Why not dynamically populate the DataGridView like we did with the recordset?

Again, we could but it would make the DataSet, DataTable and DataView a rather pointless pursuit and waste effort of time. There is also another idea you may want to consider: Create a module that does nothing but covert from one type of resource to another.

With respect to the DataSet, DataTable and DataView, they all share a common entity, the Datatable. As I have already shown, the Dataset is a collection of DataTables:

The DataTable added to the DataSet

```
Dim ds as new System.Data.DataSet
Dim dt as new System.Data.DataTable
ds.Tables.Add(dt)
```

The Datatable as a standalone

```
Dim dt as new System.Data.DataTable
```

The Datatable creating a DataView

```
Dim dt as new System.Data.DataTable
Dim dv as System.Data.DataTable = dt.DefaultView
```

So, if you use the DataTable, you have all three done at the same time and will be less code to write, too. Furthermore, we have other ways to convert a Recordset into more than a DataSet, DataTable or DataView. We can create arrays, Dictionary objects, ISAMs, delimited text files and Excel Worksheets.

And that brings us back to why do all the conversions if the recordset can stand on its own 2 feet.

The answer, we're not always going to be doing recordsets. WbemScripting is a perfect example of what is meant. Unless you take the data and put it into an Access Database, it needs to be converted over to something other than WMI to populate the DataGridView through its DataSource.

This concept weighs in heavily when working with WPF.

Working with the Listview
A control without a DataSource to bind to.

The Listview control has no DataSource to which you can directly bind your data to. So, the code needs to dynamically populate it.

Below is the request code:

```
    Private Sub Button1_Click(sender As System.Object, e As
System.EventArgs) Handles Button1.Click
        Dim cn As Object = CreateObject("ADODB.Connection")
        cn.ConnectionString =
"Provider=Microsoft.Jet.OleDb.4.0;Data Source=C:\Program Files
(x86)\Microsoft Visual Studio\VB98\NWind.mdb"
        cn.Open("")

        Dim rs As Object = CreateObject("ADODB.Recordset")
        rs.ActiveConnection = cn
        rs.CursorLocation = 3
        rs.LockType = 3
        rs.Source = "Select * From Products"
        rs.Open()

        populate_Listview_Using_A_Recordset(rs, ListView1,
"Single Line Horizontal")

    End Sub

    Private Sub Button2_Click(sender As System.Object, e As
System.EventArgs) Handles Button2.Click
        Dim cn As Object = CreateObject("ADODB.Connection")
        cn.ConnectionString =
"Provider=Microsoft.Jet.OleDb.4.0;Data Source=C:\Program Files
(x86)\Microsoft Visual Studio\VB98\NWind.mdb"
        cn.Open("")

        Dim rs As Object = CreateObject("ADODB.Recordset")
        rs.ActiveConnection = cn
        rs.CursorLocation = 3
        rs.LockType = 3
```

```vb
        rs.Source = "Select * From Products"
        rs.Open()

        populate_Listview_Using_A_Recordset(rs, ListView1, "Multi
Line Horizontal")
    End Sub

    Private Sub Button3_Click(sender As System.Object, e As
System.EventArgs) Handles Button3.Click
        Dim cn As Object = CreateObject("ADODB.Connection")
        cn.ConnectionString =
"Provider=Microsoft.Jet.OleDb.4.0;Data Source=C:\Program Files
(x86)\Microsoft Visual Studio\VB98\NWind.mdb"
        cn.Open("")

        Dim rs As Object = CreateObject("ADODB.Recordset")
        rs.ActiveConnection = cn
        rs.CursorLocation = 3
        rs.LockType = 3
        rs.Source = "Select * From Products"
        rs.Open()

        populate_Listview_Using_A_Recordset(rs, ListView1,
"Single Line Vertical")
    End Sub

    Private Sub Button4_Click(sender As System.Object, e As
System.EventArgs) Handles Button4.Click
        Dim cn As Object = CreateObject("ADODB.Connection")
        cn.ConnectionString =
"Provider=Microsoft.Jet.OleDb.4.0;Data Source=C:\Program Files
(x86)\Microsoft Visual Studio\VB98\NWind.mdb"
        cn.Open("")

        Dim rs As Object = CreateObject("ADODB.Recordset")
        rs.ActiveConnection = cn
        rs.CursorLocation = 3
        rs.LockType = 3
        rs.Source = "Select * From Products"
        rs.Open()

        populate_Listview_Using_A_Recordset(rs, ListView1, "Multi
Line Vertical")

    End Sub
```

And the receiving code:

```vb
Public Sub populate_Listview_Using_A_Recordset(ByVal rs As
Object, ByVal ListView1 As ListView, ByVal Orientation As String)

    Dim x As Integer = 0
    Dim y As Integer = 0

    ListView1.Items.Clear()

    Select Case Orientation

        Case "Single Line Horizontal"

            For x = 0 To rs.Fields.Count - 1
                ListView1.Columns.Add(rs.Fields(x).Name)
            Next
            rs.MoveFirst()
            Dim li As ListViewItem
            For x = 0 To rs.Fields.Count - 1

                If x = 0 Then

                    Try
                        li =
ListView1.Items.Add(rs.Fields(x).Value)
                    Catch ex As Exception
                        li = ListView1.Items.Add("")
                    End Try

                Else

                    Try
                        li.SubItems.Add(rs.Fields(x).Value)
                    Catch ex As Exception
                        li.SubItems.Add("")
                    End Try

                End If

            Next

        Case "Multi Line Horizontal"
```

```vbnet
            For x = 0 To rs.Fields.Count - 1
                ListView1.Columns.Add(rs.Fields(x).Name)
            Next
            rs.MoveFirst()
            Dim li As ListViewItem
            rs.MoveFirst()
            Do While rs.EOF = False
                For x = 0 To rs.Fields.Count - 1

                    If x = 0 Then

                        Try
                            li =
ListView1.Items.Add(rs.Fields(x).Value)
                        Catch ex As Exception
                            li = ListView1.Items.Add("")
                        End Try

                    Else

                        Try

li.SubItems.Add(rs.Fields(x).Value)
                        Catch ex As Exception
                            li.SubItems.Add("")
                        End Try

                    End If

                Next
                rs.MoveNext()
            Loop

        Case "Single Line Vertical"

            ListView1.Columns.Add("Property Name")
            ListView1.Columns.Add("Property Value")

            Dim li As ListViewItem


            For x = 0 To rs.Fields.Count - 1
                li = ListView1.Items.Add(rs.Fields(x).Name)
                Try
```

```
                    li.SubItems.Add(rs.Fields(x).Value)
                Catch ex As Exception
                    li.SubItems.Add("")
                End Try
            Next

        Case "Multi Line Vertical"

            ListView1.Columns.Add(" Property Name")
            Dim li As ListViewItem
            For y = 0 To rs.RecordCount - 1
                ListView1.Columns.Add("Row" & y)
            Next

            For x = 0 To rs.Fields.Count - 1
                li = ListView1.Items.Add(rs.Fields(x).Name)
                rs.MoveFirst()
                Do While rs.Eof = False
                    Try
                        li.SubItems.Add(rs.Fields(x).Value)
                    Catch ex As Exception
                        li.SubItems.Add("")
                    End Try
                    rs.MoveNext()
                Loop
            Next

    End Select

End Sub
```

The single line Horizontal looks like this:

The multi-line horizontal looks like this:

ProductID	Product...	Supplier...	Categor...	Quantity...	UnitPrice	UnitsIn...	UnitsOn...	Reorder...	Disconti
1	Chai	1	1	10 boxe...	18	39	0	10	False
2	Chang	1	1	24 - 12	19	17	40	25	False
3	Aniseed...	1	2	12 - 550...	10	13	70	25	False
4	Chef An...	2	2	48 - 6 o...	22	53	0	0	False
5	Chef An...	2	2	36 boxes	21.35	0	0	0	True
6	Grandm...	3	2	12 - 8 o...	25	120	0	25	False
7	Uncle B...	3	7	12 - 1 lb...	30	15	0	10	False
8	Northw...	3	2	12 - 12 ...	40	6	0	0	False
9	Mishi K...	4	6	18 - 500...	97	29	0	0	True
10	Ikura	4	8	12 - 200...	31	31	0	0	False
11	Queso ...	5	4	1 kg pkg.	21	22	30	30	False
12	Queso ...	5	4	10 - 500...	38	86	0	0	False
13	Konbu	6	8	2 kg box	6	24	0	5	False
14	Tofu	6	7	40 - 100...	23.25	35	0	0	False
15	Genen ...	6	2	24 - 250...	15.5	39	0	5	False
16	Pavlova	7	3	32 - 500...	17.45	29	0	10	False
17	Alice M...	7	6	20 - 1 k...	39	0	0	0	True
18	Camarv...	7	8	16 kg p...	62.5	42	0	0	False
19	Teatime...	8	3	10 boxe...	9.2	25	0	5	False
20	Sir Rod...	8	3	30 gift b...	81	40	0	0	False
21	Sir Rod...	8	3	24 pkgs...	10	3	40	5	False
22	Gustaf's...	9	5	24 - 500...	21	104	0	25	False
23	Tunnbröd	9	5	12 - 250...	9	61	0	25	False
24	Guaran...	10	1	12 - 355...	4.5	20	0	0	True
25	NuNuC...	11	3	20 - 450...	14	76	0	30	False
26	Gumbär...	11	3	100 - 25...	31.23	15	0	0	False

SLH

MLH

SLV

MLV

The single line vertical looks like this:

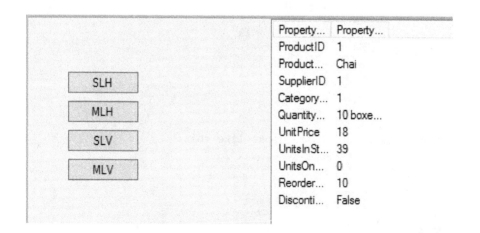

And the multi-line vertical looks like this:

Propert...	Row0	Row1	Row2	Row3	Row4	Row5	Row6
ProductID	1	2	3	4	5	6	7
Product...	Chai	Chang	Aniseed...	Chef An...	Chef An...	Grandm...	Uncle B...
SupplierID	1	1	1	2	2	3	3
Category...	1	1	2	2	2	2	7
Quantity...	10 boxe...	24 - 12 ...	12 - 550...	48 - 6 o...	36 boxes	12 - 8 o...	12 - 1 lb...
UnitPrice	18	19	10	22	21.35	25	30
UnitsInSt...	39	17	13	53	0	120	15
UnitsOn...	0	40	70	0	0	0	0
Reorder...	10	25	25	0	0	25	10
Disconti...	False	False	False	False	True	False	False

SLH

MLH

SLV

MLV

Listview and DataSet

The code that makes the request:

```
    Private Sub Button1_Click(sender As System.Object, e As
System.EventArgs) Handles Button1.Click

        Dim cn As ADODB.Connection = New ADODB.Connection
        cn.ConnectionString =
"Provider=Microsoft.Jet.OleDb.4.0;Data Source=C:\Program Files
(x86)\Microsoft Visual Studio\VB98\NWind.mdb"
        cn.Open()

        Dim rs As ADODB.Recordset = New ADODB.Recordset
        rs.ActiveConnection = cn
        rs.CursorLocation = 3
        rs.LockType = 3
        rs.let_Source("Select * From Products")
        rs.Open()

        Dim Da As New System.Data.OleDb.OleDbDataAdapter
        Dim ds As New System.Data.DataSet
        Da.Fill(ds, rs, "Products")

        populate_Listview_Using_A_DataSet(ds, ListView1, "Single
Line Horizontal")

    End Sub
```

```vbnet
    Private Sub Button2_Click(sender As System.Object, e As
System.EventArgs) Handles Button2.Click

        Dim cn As ADODB.Connection = New ADODB.Connection
        cn.ConnectionString =
"Provider=Microsoft.Jet.OleDb.4.0;Data Source=C:\Program Files
(x86)\Microsoft Visual Studio\VB98\NWind.mdb"
        cn.Open()

        Dim rs As ADODB.Recordset = New ADODB.Recordset
        rs.ActiveConnection = cn
        rs.CursorLocation = 3
        rs.LockType = 3
        rs.let_Source("Select * From Products")
        rs.Open()

        Dim Da As New System.Data.OleDb.OleDbDataAdapter
        Dim ds As New System.Data.DataSet
        Da.Fill(ds, rs, "Products")

        populate_Listview_Using_A_DataSet(ds, ListView1, "Multi
Line Horizontal")

    End Sub

    Private Sub Button3_Click(sender As System.Object, e As
System.EventArgs) Handles Button3.Click

        Dim cn As ADODB.Connection = New ADODB.Connection
        cn.ConnectionString =
"Provider=Microsoft.Jet.OleDb.4.0;Data Source=C:\Program Files
(x86)\Microsoft Visual Studio\VB98\NWind.mdb"
        cn.Open()

        Dim rs As ADODB.Recordset = New ADODB.Recordset
        rs.ActiveConnection = cn
        rs.CursorLocation = 3
        rs.LockType = 3
        rs.let_Source("Select * From Products")
        rs.Open()

        Dim Da As New System.Data.OleDb.OleDbDataAdapter
        Dim ds As New System.Data.DataSet
        Da.Fill(ds, rs, "Products")
```

```vb
        populate_Listview_Using_A_DataSet(ds, ListView1, "Single
Line Vertical")

    End Sub

    Private Sub Button4_Click(sender As System.Object, e As
System.EventArgs) Handles Button4.Click


        Dim cn As ADODB.Connection = New ADODB.Connection
        cn.ConnectionString =
"Provider=Microsoft.Jet.OleDb.4.0;Data Source=C:\Program Files
(x86)\Microsoft Visual Studio\VB98\NWind.mdb"
        cn.Open()

        Dim rs As ADODB.Recordset = New ADODB.Recordset
        rs.ActiveConnection = cn
        rs.CursorLocation = 3
        rs.LockType = 3
        rs.let_Source("Select * From Products")
        rs.Open()

        Dim Da As New System.Data.OleDb.OleDbDataAdapter
        Dim ds As New System.Data.DataSet
        Da.Fill(ds, rs, "Products")

        populate_Listview_Using_A_DataSet(ds, ListView1, "Multi
Line Vertical")

    End Sub
```

The code that receives the request:


```vb
    Public Sub populate_Listview_Using_A_DataSet(ByVal Ds As
DataSet, ByVal ListView1 As ListView, ByVal Orientation As
String)

        Dim x As Integer = 0
        Dim y As Integer = 0

        ListView1.Items.Clear()
        ListView1.Columns.Clear()
```

```vbnet
Select Case Orientation

    Case "Single Line Horizontal"

        For Each col As System.Data.DataColumn In
Ds.Tables(0).Columns
            ListView1.Columns.Add(col.Caption)
        Next
        Dim dr As System.Data.DataRow =
Ds.Tables(0).Rows(0)
        Dim li As ListViewItem
        For Each col As System.Data.DataColumn In
Ds.Tables(0).Columns

            If x = 0 Then

                Try
                    li =
ListView1.Items.Add(dr.Item(col.Caption))
                Catch ex As Exception
                    li = ListView1.Items.Add("")
                End Try

            Else

                Try
                    li.SubItems.Add(dr.Item(col.Caption))
                Catch ex As Exception
                    li.SubItems.Add("")
                End Try

            End If

            x = 1

        Next

    Case "Multi Line Horizontal"

        For Each col As System.Data.DataColumn In
Ds.Tables(0).Columns
            ListView1.Columns.Add(col.Caption)
        Next
```

```vbnet
                Dim li As ListViewItem = Nothing

                For Each dr As System.Data.DataRow In
Ds.Tables(0).Rows
                    For Each col As System.Data.DataColumn In
Ds.Tables(0).Columns
                        If x = 0 Then
                            Try
                                li =
ListView1.Items.Add(dr.Item(col.Caption))
                            Catch ex As Exception
                                li = ListView1.Items.Add("")
                            End Try
                        Else
                            Try

li.SubItems.Add(dr.Item(col.Caption))
                            Catch ex As Exception
                                li.SubItems.Add("")
                            End Try

                        End If
                        x = x + 1
                    Next
                    x = 0
                Next

            Case "Single Line Vertical"

                ListView1.Columns.Add("Property Name")
                ListView1.Columns.Add("Property Value")

                Dim li As ListViewItem

                Dim dr As System.Data.DataRow =
Ds.Tables(0).Rows(0)
                For Each col As System.Data.DataColumn In
Ds.Tables(0).Columns
                    li = ListView1.Items.Add(col.Caption)
                    Try
                        li.SubItems.Add(dr.Item(col.Caption))
                    Catch ex As Exception
                        li.SubItems.Add("")
                    End Try
                Next
```

```vb
        Case "Multi Line Vertical"

                ListView1.Columns.Add(" Property Name")
                Dim li As ListViewItem
                For Each row As System.Data.DataRow In
Ds.Tables(0).Rows
                        ListView1.Columns.Add("Row" & y)
                Next

                For Each col As System.Data.DataColumn In
Ds.Tables(0).Columns
                        li = ListView1.Items.Add(col.Caption)
                        For Each dr As System.Data.DataRow In
Ds.Tables(0).Rows
                            Try
                                li.SubItems.Add(dr.Item(col.Caption))
                            Catch ex As Exception
                                li.SubItems.Add("")
                            End Try
                        Next
                Next

        End Select

    End Sub
```

The code that makes the request:

```vb
    Private Sub Button1_Click(sender As System.Object, e As
System.EventArgs) Handles Button1.Click

        Dim cn As ADODB.Connection = New ADODB.Connection
        cn.ConnectionString =
"Provider=Microsoft.Jet.OleDb.4.0;Data Source=C:\Program Files
(x86)\Microsoft Visual Studio\VB98\NWind.mdb"
        cn.Open()

        Dim rs As ADODB.Recordset = New ADODB.Recordset
        rs.ActiveConnection = cn
        rs.CursorLocation = 3
        rs.LockType = 3
        rs.let_Source("Select * From Products")
```

```vb
        rs.Open()

        Dim Da As New System.Data.OleDb.OleDbDataAdapter
        Dim dt As New System.Data.DataTable
        Da.Fill(dt, rs)

        populate_Listview_Using_A_DataTable(dt, ListView1,
"Single Line Horizontal")

    End Sub

    Private Sub Button2_Click(sender As System.Object, e As
System.EventArgs) Handles Button2.Click

        Dim cn As ADODB.Connection = New ADODB.Connection
        cn.ConnectionString =
"Provider=Microsoft.Jet.OleDb.4.0;Data Source=C:\Program Files
(x86)\Microsoft Visual Studio\VB98\NWind.mdb"
        cn.Open()

        Dim rs As ADODB.Recordset = New ADODB.Recordset
        rs.ActiveConnection = cn
        rs.CursorLocation = 3
        rs.LockType = 3
        rs.let_Source("Select * From Products")
        rs.Open()

        Dim Da As New System.Data.OleDb.OleDbDataAdapter
        Dim dt As New System.Data.DataTable
        Da.Fill(dt, rs)

        populate_Listview_Using_A_DataTable(dt, ListView1, "Multi
Line Horizontal")

    End Sub

    Private Sub Button3_Click(sender As System.Object, e As
System.EventArgs) Handles Button3.Click

        Dim cn As ADODB.Connection = New ADODB.Connection
        cn.ConnectionString =
"Provider=Microsoft.Jet.OleDb.4.0;Data Source=C:\Program Files
(x86)\Microsoft Visual Studio\VB98\NWind.mdb"
        cn.Open()
```

```vb
        Dim rs As ADODB.Recordset = New ADODB.Recordset
        rs.ActiveConnection = cn
        rs.CursorLocation = 3
        rs.LockType = 3
        rs.let_Source("Select * From Products")
        rs.Open()

        Dim Da As New System.Data.OleDb.OleDbDataAdapter
        Dim dt As New System.Data.DataTable
        Da.Fill(dt, rs)

        populate_Listview_Using_A_DataTable(dt, ListView1,
"Single Line Vertical")

    End Sub

    Private Sub Button4_Click(sender As System.Object, e As
System.EventArgs) Handles Button4.Click


        Dim cn As ADODB.Connection = New ADODB.Connection
        cn.ConnectionString =
"Provider=Microsoft.Jet.OleDb.4.0;Data Source=C:\Program Files
(x86)\Microsoft Visual Studio\VB98\NWind.mdb"
        cn.Open()

        Dim rs As ADODB.Recordset = New ADODB.Recordset
        rs.ActiveConnection = cn
        rs.CursorLocation = 3
        rs.LockType = 3
        rs.let_Source("Select * From Products")
        rs.Open()

        Dim Da As New System.Data.OleDb.OleDbDataAdapter
        Dim dt As New System.Data.DataTable
        Da.Fill(dt, rs)

        populate_Listview_Using_A_DataTable(dt, ListView1, "Multi
Line Vertical")

    End Sub
```

The code that receives the request:

```vb
    Public Sub populate_Listview_Using_A_DataTable(ByVal Dt As
DataTable, ByVal ListView1 As ListView, ByVal Orientation As
String)

        Dim x As Integer = 0
        Dim y As Integer = 0

        ListView1.Items.Clear()
        ListView1.Columns.Clear()

        Select Case Orientation

            Case "Single Line Horizontal"

                For Each col As System.Data.DataColumn In
Dt.Columns
                    ListView1.Columns.Add(col.Caption)
                Next
                Dim dr As System.Data.DataRow = Dt.Rows(0)
                Dim li As ListViewItem
                For Each col As System.Data.DataColumn In
Dt.Columns

                    If x = 0 Then

                        Try
                            li =
ListView1.Items.Add(dr.Item(col.Caption))
                        Catch ex As Exception
                            li = ListView1.Items.Add("")
                        End Try

                    Else

                        Try
                            li.SubItems.Add(dr.Item(col.Caption))
                        Catch ex As Exception
                            li.SubItems.Add("")
                        End Try

                    End If
```

```vbnet
                        x = 1

                Next

          Case "Multi Line Horizontal"

                For Each col As System.Data.DataColumn In
Dt.Columns
                        ListView1.Columns.Add(col.Caption)
                Next

                Dim li As ListViewItem = Nothing

                For Each dr As System.Data.DataRow In Dt.Rows
                        For Each col As System.Data.DataColumn In
Dt.Columns
                                If x = 0 Then
                                        Try
                                                li =
ListView1.Items.Add(dr.Item(col.Caption))
                                        Catch ex As Exception
                                                li = ListView1.Items.Add("")
                                        End Try
                                Else
                                        Try

li.SubItems.Add(dr.Item(col.Caption))
                                        Catch ex As Exception
                                                li.SubItems.Add("")
                                        End Try

                                End If
                                x = x + 1
                        Next
                        x = 0
                Next

          Case "Single Line Vertical"

                ListView1.Columns.Add("Property Name")
                ListView1.Columns.Add("Property Value")

                Dim li As ListViewItem
```

```vbnet
            Dim dr As System.Data.DataRow = Dt.Rows(0)
            For Each col As System.Data.DataColumn In
Dt.Columns

                li = ListView1.Items.Add(col.Caption)
                Try
                    li.SubItems.Add(dr.Item(col.Caption))
                Catch ex As Exception
                    li.SubItems.Add("")
                End Try
            Next

        Case "Multi Line Vertical"

            ListView1.Columns.Add(" Property Name")
            Dim li As ListViewItem
            For Each row As System.Data.DataRow In Dt.Rows
                ListView1.Columns.Add("Row" & y)
            Next

            For Each col As System.Data.DataColumn In
Dt.Columns

                li = ListView1.Items.Add(col.Caption)
                For Each dr As System.Data.DataRow In Dt.Rows
                    Try
                        li.SubItems.Add(dr.Item(col.Caption))
                    Catch ex As Exception
                        li.SubItems.Add("")
                    End Try
                Next
            Next

        End Select

    End Sub
```

Listview and DataView

The code that creates the request:

```vb
    Private Sub Button1_Click(sender As System.Object, e As
System.EventArgs) Handles Button1.Click

        Dim cn As ADODB.Connection = New ADODB.Connection
        cn.ConnectionString =
"Provider=Microsoft.Jet.OleDb.4.0;Data Source=C:\Program Files
(x86)\Microsoft Visual Studio\VB98\NWind.mdb"
        cn.Open()

        Dim rs As ADODB.Recordset = New ADODB.Recordset
        rs.ActiveConnection = cn
        rs.CursorLocation = 3
        rs.LockType = 3
        rs.let_Source("Select * From Products")
        rs.Open()

        Dim Da As New System.Data.OleDb.OleDbDataAdapter
        Dim dt As New System.Data.DataTable
        Da.Fill(dt, rs)

        populate_Listview_Using_A_DataView(dt.DefaultView,
ListView1, "Single Line Horizontal")

    End Sub

    Private Sub Button2_Click(sender As System.Object, e As
System.EventArgs) Handles Button2.Click

        Dim cn As ADODB.Connection = New ADODB.Connection
        cn.ConnectionString =
"Provider=Microsoft.Jet.OleDb.4.0;Data Source=C:\Program Files
(x86)\Microsoft Visual Studio\VB98\NWind.mdb"
        cn.Open()

        Dim rs As ADODB.Recordset = New ADODB.Recordset
        rs.ActiveConnection = cn
        rs.CursorLocation = 3
        rs.LockType = 3
        rs.let_Source("Select * From Products")
        rs.Open()

        Dim Da As New System.Data.OleDb.OleDbDataAdapter
        Dim dt As New System.Data.DataTable
        Da.Fill(dt, rs)
```

```vb
        populate_Listview_Using_A_DataView(dt.DefaultView,
ListView1, "Multi Line Horizontal")

    End Sub

    Private Sub Button3_Click(sender As System.Object, e As
System.EventArgs) Handles Button3.Click

        Dim cn As ADODB.Connection = New ADODB.Connection
        cn.ConnectionString =
"Provider=Microsoft.Jet.OleDb.4.0;Data Source=C:\Program Files
(x86)\Microsoft Visual Studio\VB98\NWind.mdb"
        cn.Open()

        Dim rs As ADODB.Recordset = New ADODB.Recordset
        rs.ActiveConnection = cn
        rs.CursorLocation = 3
        rs.LockType = 3
        rs.let_Source("Select * From Products")
        rs.Open()

        Dim Da As New System.Data.OleDb.OleDbDataAdapter
        Dim dt As New System.Data.DataTable
        Da.Fill(dt, rs)

        populate_Listview_Using_A_DataView(dt.DefaultView,
ListView1, "Single Line Vertical")

    End Sub

    Private Sub Button4_Click(sender As System.Object, e As
System.EventArgs) Handles Button4.Click


        Dim cn As ADODB.Connection = New ADODB.Connection
        cn.ConnectionString =
"Provider=Microsoft.Jet.OleDb.4.0;Data Source=C:\Program Files
(x86)\Microsoft Visual Studio\VB98\NWind.mdb"
        cn.Open()

        Dim rs As ADODB.Recordset = New ADODB.Recordset
        rs.ActiveConnection = cn
        rs.CursorLocation = 3
        rs.LockType = 3
        rs.let_Source("Select * From Products")
```

```vbnet
        rs.Open()

        Dim Da As New System.Data.OleDb.OleDbDataAdapter
        Dim dt As New System.Data.DataTable
        Da.Fill(dt, rs)

        populate_Listview_Using_A_DataView(dt.DefaultView,
ListView1, "Multi Line Vertical")

    End Sub
```

The code that receives the request:

```vbnet
    Public Sub populate_Listview_Using_A_DataView(ByVal dv As
System.Data.DataView, ByVal ListView1 As ListView, ByVal
Orientation As String)

        Dim x As Integer = 0
        Dim y As Integer = 0

        ListView1.Items.Clear()
        ListView1.Columns.Clear()

        Select Case Orientation

            Case "Single Line Horizontal"

                For Each col As System.Data.DataColumn In
dv.Table.Columns
                    ListView1.Columns.Add(col.Caption)
                Next
                Dim dr As System.Data.DataRow = dv.Table.Rows(0)
                Dim li As ListViewItem
                For Each col As System.Data.DataColumn In
dv.Table.Columns

                    If x = 0 Then

                        Try
                            li =
ListView1.Items.Add(dr.Item(col.Caption))
```

```vbnet
                        Catch ex As Exception
                            li = ListView1.Items.Add("")
                        End Try

                    Else

                        Try
                            li.SubItems.Add(dr.Item(col.Caption))
                        Catch ex As Exception
                            li.SubItems.Add("")
                        End Try

                    End If

                    x = 1

                Next

            Case "Multi Line Horizontal"

                For Each col As System.Data.DataColumn In
dv.Table.Columns
                    ListView1.Columns.Add(col.Caption)
                Next

                Dim li As ListViewItem = Nothing

                For Each dr As System.Data.DataRow In
dv.Table.Rows
                    For Each col As System.Data.DataColumn In
dv.Table.Columns
                        If x = 0 Then
                            Try
                                li =
ListView1.Items.Add(dr.Item(col.Caption))
                            Catch ex As Exception
                                li = ListView1.Items.Add("")
                            End Try
                        Else
                            Try

li.SubItems.Add(dr.Item(col.Caption))
                            Catch ex As Exception
                                li.SubItems.Add("")
                            End Try
```

```vbnet
                    End If
                    x = x + 1
                Next
                x = 0
            Next

        Case "Single Line Vertical"

            ListView1.Columns.Add("Property Name")
            ListView1.Columns.Add("Property Value")

            Dim li As ListViewItem

            Dim dr As System.Data.DataRow = dv.Table.Rows(0)
            For Each col As System.Data.DataColumn In
dv.Table.Columns
                li = ListView1.Items.Add(col.Caption)
                Try
                    li.SubItems.Add(dr.Item(col.Caption))
                Catch ex As Exception
                    li.SubItems.Add("")
                End Try
            Next

        Case "Multi Line Vertical"

            ListView1.Columns.Add(" Property Name")
            Dim li As ListViewItem
            For Each row As System.Data.DataRow In
dv.Table.Rows
                ListView1.Columns.Add("Row" & y)
            Next

            For Each col As System.Data.DataColumn In
dv.Table.Columns
                li = ListView1.Items.Add(col.Caption)
                For Each dr As System.Data.DataRow In
dv.Table.Rows
                    Try
                        li.SubItems.Add(dr.Item(col.Caption))
                    Catch ex As Exception
                        li.SubItems.Add("")
                    End Try
                Next
```

```
            Next

        End Select

    End Sub
```

MSFlexgrid

Like VB6 the MSFlexgrid is still around and still as awesome as ever!

Below is the code that makes the requests.

```
    Private Sub Button1_Click(sender As System.Object, e As
System.EventArgs) Handles Button1.Click
        Dim cn As Object = CreateObject("ADODB.Connection")
        cn.ConnectionString =
"Provider=Microsoft.Jet.OleDb.4.0;Data Source=C:\Program Files
(x86)\Microsoft Visual Studio\VB98\NWind.mdb"
        cn.Open("")

        Dim rs As Object = CreateObject("ADODB.Recordset")
        rs.ActiveConnection = cn
        rs.CursorLocation = 3
        rs.LockType = 3
        rs.Source = "Select * From Products"
        rs.Open()

        populate_Listview_Using_A_Recordset(rs, ListView1,
"Single Line Horizontal")

    End Sub

    Private Sub Button2_Click(sender As System.Object, e As
System.EventArgs) Handles Button2.Click
        Dim cn As Object = CreateObject("ADODB.Connection")
```

```vbnet
        cn.ConnectionString =
"Provider=Microsoft.Jet.OleDb.4.0;Data Source=C:\Program Files
(x86)\Microsoft Visual Studio\VB98\NWind.mdb"
        cn.Open("")

        Dim rs As Object = CreateObject("ADODB.Recordset")
        rs.ActiveConnection = cn
        rs.CursorLocation = 3
        rs.LockType = 3
        rs.Source = "Select * From Products"
        rs.Open()

        populate_Listview_Using_A_Recordset(rs, ListView1, "Multi
Line Horizontal")
    End Sub

    Private Sub Button3_Click(sender As System.Object, e As
System.EventArgs) Handles Button3.Click
        Dim cn As Object = CreateObject("ADODB.Connection")
        cn.ConnectionString =
"Provider=Microsoft.Jet.OleDb.4.0;Data Source=C:\Program Files
(x86)\Microsoft Visual Studio\VB98\NWind.mdb"
        cn.Open("")

        Dim rs As Object = CreateObject("ADODB.Recordset")
        rs.ActiveConnection = cn
        rs.CursorLocation = 3
        rs.LockType = 3
        rs.Source = "Select * From Products"
        rs.Open()

        populate_Listview_Using_A_Recordset(rs, ListView1,
"Single Line Vertical")
    End Sub

    Private Sub Button4_Click(sender As System.Object, e As
System.EventArgs) Handles Button4.Click
        Dim cn As Object = CreateObject("ADODB.Connection")
        cn.ConnectionString =
"Provider=Microsoft.Jet.OleDb.4.0;Data Source=C:\Program Files
(x86)\Microsoft Visual Studio\VB98\NWind.mdb"
        cn.Open("")

        Dim rs As Object = CreateObject("ADODB.Recordset")
        rs.ActiveConnection = cn
```

```
        rs.CursorLocation = 3
        rs.LockType = 3
        rs.Source = "Select * From Products"
        rs.Open()

        populate_Listview_Using_A_Recordset(rs, ListView1, "Multi
Line Vertical")

    End Sub
```

Below is the Recordset code that accepts the requests:

```
    Public Sub populate_MSFlexgrid_Using_A_Recordset(ByVal rs As
Object, ByVal MSFlexgrid1 As AxMSFlexGridLib.AxMSFlexGrid, ByVal
Orientation As String)

        Dim x As Integer = 0
        Dim y As Integer = 0

        Select Case Orientation

            Case "Single Line Horizontal"

                MSFlexgrid1.Rows = 2
                MSFlexgrid1.Cols = rs.Fields.Count + 1

                For x = 0 To rs.Fields.Count - 1
                    MSFlexgrid1.set_TextMatrix(0, x + 1,
rs.Fields(x).Name)
                Next

                rs.MoveFirst()
                For x = 0 To rs.Fields.Count - 1
                    Try
                        MSFlexgrid1.set_TextMatrix(1, x + 1,
rs.Fields(x).Value)
                    Catch ex As Exception
                        MSFlexgrid1.set_TextMatrix(1, x + 1, "")
                    End Try
                Next
```

```vbnet
        Case "Multi Line Horizontal"


                MSFlexgrid1.Rows = rs.RecordCount + 1
                MSFlexgrid1.Cols = rs.Fields.Count + 1

                For x = 0 To rs.Fields.Count - 1
                    MSFlexgrid1.set_TextMatrix(0, x + 1,
rs.Fields(x).Name)
                Next

                For x = 0 To rs.Fields.Count - 1
                    rs.MoveFirst()
                    y = 0
                    Do While rs.Eof = False

                        Try
                            MSFlexgrid1.set_TextMatrix(y + 1, x +
1, rs.Fields(x).Value)
                        Catch ex As Exception
                            MSFlexgrid1.set_TextMatrix(y + 1, x +
1, "")
                        End Try
                        y = y + 1
                        rs.MoveNext()
                    Loop
                Next

            Case "Single Line Vertical"


                MSFlexgrid1.Cols = 3
                MSFlexgrid1.Rows = rs.Fields.Count + 1

                MSFlexgrid1.set_TextMatrix(0, 1, "Property Name")
                MSFlexgrid1.set_TextMatrix(0, 2, "Property
Value")

                rs.MoveFirst()
                For x = 0 To rs.Fields.Count - 1
                    MSFlexgrid1.set_TextMatrix(x + 1, 1,
rs.Fields(x).Name)
                    Try
```

```
                        MSFlexgrid1.set_TextMatrix(x + 1, 2,
rs.Fields(x).Value)
                    Catch ex As Exception
                        MSFlexgrid1.set_TextMatrix(x + 1, 2, "")
                    End Try
                Next


        Case "Multi Line Vertical"

            MSFlexgrid1.set_TextMatrix(0, 1, "Property Name")

            MSFlexgrid1.Cols = rs.RecordCount + 1
            MSFlexgrid1.Rows = rs.Fields.Count + 1


            For y = 0 To rs.RecordCount - 1
                MSFlexgrid1.set_TextMatrix(0, y + 1, "Row" &
y)
            Next

            For x = 0 To rs.Fields.Count - 1
                MSFlexgrid1.set_TextMatrix(x + 1, 0,
rs.Fields(x).Name)
                rs.MoveFirst()
                y = 0
                Do While rs.Eof = False
                    Try
                        MSFlexgrid1.set_TextMatrix(x + 1, y +
1, rs.Fields(x).Value)
                    Catch ex As Exception
                        MSFlexgrid1.set_TextMatrix(x + 1, y +
1, "")
                    End Try
                    y = y + 1
                    rs.MoveNext()
                Loop
            Next

    End Select


    End Sub
```

The single line horizontal view looks like this:

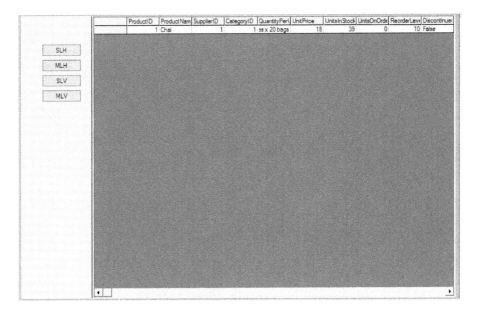

The multi-line horizontal looks like this:

ProductID	ProductNam	SupplierID	CategoryID	QuantityPerl	UnitPrice	UnitsInStock	UnitsOnOrde	ReorderLeve	Discontin
1	Chai	1	1	3s x 20 bags	18	39	0	10	False
2	Chang	1	1	12 oz bottles	19	17	40	25	False
3	Aniseed Syn	1	2	50 ml bottles	10	13	70	25	False
4	Chef Anton's	2	2	48 - 6 oz jars	22	53	0	0	False
5	Chef Anton's	2	2	36 boxes	21.35	0	0	0	True
6	Grandma's E	3	2	12 - 8 oz jars	25	120	0	25	False
7	Uncle Bob's	3	7	2 - 1 lb pkgs.	30	15	0	10	False
8	Northwoods	3	2	2 - 12 oz jars	40	6	0	0	False
9	Mishi Kobe l	4	6	500 g pkgs.	97	29	0	0	True
10	Ikura	4	8	- 200 ml jars	31	31	0	0	False
11	Queso Cabra	5	4	1 kg pkg.	21	22	30	30	False
12	Queso Manc	5	4	500 g pkgs.	38	86	0	0	False
13	Konbu	6	8	2 kg box	6	24	0	5	False
14	Tofu	6	7	100 g pkgs.	23.25	35	0	0	False
15	Genen Shou	6	2	50 ml bottles	15.5	39	0	5	False
16	Pavlova	7	3	500 g boxes	17.45	29	0	10	False
17	Alice Mutton	7	6	20 - 1 kg tins	39	0	0	0	True
18	Camarvon T	7	8	16 kg pkg.	62.5	42	0	0	False
19	Teatime Cho	8	3	x 12 pieces	9.2	25	0	5	False
20	Sir Rodney's	8	3	30 gift boxes	81	40	0	0	False
21	Sir Rodney's	8	3	s. x 4 pieces	10	3	40	5	False
22	Gustaf's Kna	9	5	500 g pkgs.	21	104	0	25	False
23	Tunnbröd	9	5	250 g pkgs.	9	61	0	25	False
24	Guaraná Far	10	1	355 ml cans	4.5	20	0	0	True
25	NuNuCa Nu	11	3	50 g glasses	14	76	0	30	False
26	Gumbär Gun	11	3	- 250 g bags	31.23	15	0	0	False
27	Schoggi Sch	11	3	100 g pieces	43.9	49	0	30	False
28	Rössle Saue	12	7	- 825 g cans	45.6	26	0	0	True
29	Thüringer Ro	12	6	x 30 sausage.	123.79	0	0	0	True
30	Nord-Ost Ma	13	8	00 g glasses	25.89	10	0	15	False
31	Gorgonzola	14	4	- 100 g pkgs	12.5	0	70	20	False

SLH
MLH
SLV
MLV

The single line vertical looks like this:

Property Nar	Property Valt
ProductID	1
ProductNam	Chai
SupplierID	1
CategoryID	1
QuantityPerl	3s x 20 bags
UnitPrice	18
UnitsInStock	39
UnitsOnOrde	0
ReorderLeve	10
Discontinued	False

SLH

MLH

SLV

MLV

The multi-line vertical looks like this:

	Row0	Row1	Row2	Row3	Row4	Row5	Row6	Row7	Row8	Row9
ProductID	1	2	3	4	5	6	7	8	9	10
ProductNam	Chai	Chang	Aniseed Syr	Chef Anton't	Chef Anton's	Grandma's E	Uncle Bob's	Northwoods	Mishi Kobe I	Ikura
SupplierID	1	1	1	2	2	3	3	3	4	4
CategoryID	1	1	2	2	2	2	7	2	6	8
QuantityPerl	ss x 20 bags	12 oz bottles	50 ml bottles	48 - 6 oz jars	36 boxes	12 - 8 oz jars	2 - 1 lb pkgs.	2 - 12 oz jars	500 g pkgs.	- 200 ml jars
UnitPrice	18	19	10	22	21.35	25	30	40	97	31
UnitsInStock	39	17	13	53	0	120	15	6	29	31
UnitsOnOrde	0	40	70	0	0	0	0	0	0	0
ReorderLeve	10	25	25	0	0	25	10	0	0	0
Discontinued	False	False	False	False	True	False	False	False	True	False

SLH

MLH

SLV

MLV

MSFlexgrid and the Dataset

The code that makes the request:

```
    Private Sub Button1_Click(sender As System.Object, e As
System.EventArgs) Handles Button1.Click

        Dim cn As ADODB.Connection = New ADODB.Connection
        cn.ConnectionString =
"Provider=Microsoft.Jet.OleDb.4.0;Data Source=C:\Program Files
(x86)\Microsoft Visual Studio\VB98\NWind.mdb"
        cn.Open()

        Dim rs As ADODB.Recordset = New ADODB.Recordset
        rs.ActiveConnection = cn
        rs.CursorLocation = 3
        rs.LockType = 3
        rs.let_Source("Select * From Products")
        rs.Open()

        Dim Da As New System.Data.OleDb.OleDbDataAdapter
        Dim ds As New System.Data.DataSet
        Da.Fill(ds, rs, "Products")

        populate_MSFlexgrid_Using_A_DataSet(ds, AxMSFlexGrid1,
"Single Line Horizontal")

    End Sub

    Private Sub Button2_Click(sender As System.Object, e As
System.EventArgs) Handles Button2.Click

        Dim cn As ADODB.Connection = New ADODB.Connection
```

```vb
        cn.ConnectionString =
"Provider=Microsoft.Jet.OleDb.4.0;Data Source=C:\Program Files
(x86)\Microsoft Visual Studio\VB98\NWind.mdb"
        cn.Open()

        Dim rs As ADODB.Recordset = New ADODB.Recordset
        rs.ActiveConnection = cn
        rs.CursorLocation = 3
        rs.LockType = 3
        rs.let_Source("Select * From Products")
        rs.Open()

        Dim Da As New System.Data.OleDb.OleDbDataAdapter
        Dim ds As New System.Data.DataSet
        Da.Fill(ds, rs, "Products")

        populate_MSFlexgrid_Using_A_DataSet(ds, AxMSFlexGrid1,
"Multi Line Horizontal")

    End Sub

    Private Sub Button3_Click(sender As System.Object, e As
System.EventArgs) Handles Button3.Click

        Dim cn As ADODB.Connection = New ADODB.Connection
        cn.ConnectionString =
"Provider=Microsoft.Jet.OleDb.4.0;Data Source=C:\Program Files
(x86)\Microsoft Visual Studio\VB98\NWind.mdb"
        cn.Open()

        Dim rs As ADODB.Recordset = New ADODB.Recordset
        rs.ActiveConnection = cn
        rs.CursorLocation = 3
        rs.LockType = 3
        rs.let_Source("Select * From Products")
        rs.Open()

        Dim Da As New System.Data.OleDb.OleDbDataAdapter
        Dim ds As New System.Data.DataSet
        Da.Fill(ds, rs, "Products")

        populate_MSFlexgrid_Using_A_DataSet(ds, AxMSFlexGrid1,
"Single Line Vertical")

    End Sub
```

```vbnet
    Private Sub Button4_Click(sender As System.Object, e As
System.EventArgs) Handles Button4.Click


        Dim cn As ADODB.Connection = New ADODB.Connection
        cn.ConnectionString =
"Provider=Microsoft.Jet.OleDb.4.0;Data Source=C:\Program Files
(x86)\Microsoft Visual Studio\VB98\NWind.mdb"
        cn.Open()

        Dim rs As ADODB.Recordset = New ADODB.Recordset
        rs.ActiveConnection = cn
        rs.CursorLocation = 3
        rs.LockType = 3
        rs.let_Source("Select * From Products")
        rs.Open()

        Dim Da As New System.Data.OleDb.OleDbDataAdapter
        Dim ds As New System.Data.DataSet
        Da.Fill(ds, rs, "Products")

        populate_MSFlexgrid_Using_A_DataSet(ds, AxMSFlexGrid1,
"Multi Line Vertical")

    End Sub

The Code that receives the request:


    Public Sub populate_MSFlexgrid_Using_A_DataSet(ByVal ds As
System.Data.DataSet, ByVal MSFlexgrid1 As
AxMSFlexGridLib.AxMSFlexGrid, ByVal Orientation As String)

        Dim x As Integer = 0
        Dim y As Integer = 0

        Select Case Orientation

            Case "Single Line Horizontal"

                MSFlexgrid1.Rows = 2
                MSFlexgrid1.Cols = ds.Tables(0).Columns.Count + 1

                For x = 0 To ds.Tables(0).Columns.Count - 1
```

```vb
                    MSFlexgrid1.set_TextMatrix(0, x + 1,
ds.Tables(0).Columns(x).Caption)
                Next

                Dim dr As System.Data.DataRow =
ds.Tables(0).Rows(0)
                For x = 0 To ds.Tables(0).Columns.Count - 1
                    Try
                        MSFlexgrid1.set_TextMatrix(1, x + 1,
dr.Item(ds.Tables(0).Columns(x).Caption))
                    Catch ex As Exception
                        MSFlexgrid1.set_TextMatrix(1, x + 1, "")
                    End Try
                Next

            Case "Multi Line Horizontal"

                MSFlexgrid1.Rows = ds.Tables(0).Rows.Count + 1
                MSFlexgrid1.Cols = ds.Tables(0).Columns.Count + 1

                For x = 0 To ds.Tables(0).Columns.Count - 1
                    MSFlexgrid1.set_TextMatrix(0, x + 1,
ds.Tables(0).Columns(x).Caption)
                Next


                For y = 0 To ds.Tables(0).Rows.Count - 1
                    For x = 0 To ds.Tables(0).Columns.Count - 1
                        Try
                            MSFlexgrid1.set_TextMatrix(y + 1, x +
1, ds.Tables(0).Rows(y).Item(ds.Tables(0).Columns(x).Caption))
                        Catch ex As Exception
                            MSFlexgrid1.set_TextMatrix(y + 1, x +
1, "")
                        End Try
                    Next

                Next

            Case "Single Line Vertical"

                MSFlexgrid1.Cols = 2
                MSFlexgrid1.Rows = ds.Tables(0).Columns.Count + 2
```

```vb
            For x = 0 To ds.Tables(0).Columns.Count - 1
                MSFlexgrid1.set_TextMatrix(x + 1, 0,
ds.Tables(0).Columns(x).Caption)
            Next

            Dim dr As System.Data.DataRow =
ds.Tables(0).Rows(0)
            For x = 0 To ds.Tables(0).Columns.Count - 1
                Try
                    MSFlexgrid1.set_TextMatrix(x + 1, 1,
dr.Item(ds.Tables(0).Columns(x).Caption))
                Catch ex As Exception
                    MSFlexgrid1.set_TextMatrix(x + 1, 1, "")
                End Try
            Next


        Case "Multi Line Vertical"

            MSFlexgrid1.set_TextMatrix(0, 1, "Property Name")

            MSFlexgrid1.Cols = ds.Tables(0).Rows.Count + 1
            MSFlexgrid1.Rows = ds.Tables(0).Columns.Count + 1


            For y = 0 To ds.Tables(0).Rows.Count - 1
                MSFlexgrid1.set_TextMatrix(0, y + 1, "Row" &
y)
            Next

            For x = 0 To ds.Tables(0).Columns.Count - 1
                MSFlexgrid1.set_TextMatrix(x + 1, 0,
ds.Tables(0).Columns(x).Caption)
                For y = 0 To ds.Tables(0).Rows.Count - 1
                    Try
                        MSFlexgrid1.set_TextMatrix(x + 1, y +
1, ds.Tables(0).Rows(y).Item(ds.Tables(0).Columns(x).Caption))
                    Catch ex As Exception
                        MSFlexgrid1.set_TextMatrix(x + 1, y +
1, "")
                    End Try
                Next

            Next
```

```
        End Select


    End Sub



MSFlexGrid using a DataTable


The code that makes the requests:


    Private Sub Button1_Click(sender As System.Object, e As
System.EventArgs) Handles Button1.Click

        Dim cn As ADODB.Connection = New ADODB.Connection
        cn.ConnectionString =
"Provider=Microsoft.Jet.OleDb.4.0;Data Source=C:\Program Files
(x86)\Microsoft Visual Studio\VB98\NWind.mdb"
        cn.Open()

        Dim rs As ADODB.Recordset = New ADODB.Recordset
        rs.ActiveConnection = cn
        rs.CursorLocation = 3
        rs.LockType = 3
        rs.let_Source("Select * From Products")
        rs.Open()

        Dim Da As New System.Data.OleDb.OleDbDataAdapter
        Dim dt As New System.Data.DataTable
        Da.Fill(dt, rs)

        populate_MSFlexgrid_Using_A_DataTable(dt, AxMSFlexGrid1,
"Single Line Horizontal")

    End Sub

    Private Sub Button2_Click(sender As System.Object, e As
System.EventArgs) Handles Button2.Click

        Dim cn As ADODB.Connection = New ADODB.Connection
```

```vb
        cn.ConnectionString =
"Provider=Microsoft.Jet.OleDb.4.0;Data Source=C:\Program Files
(x86)\Microsoft Visual Studio\VB98\NWind.mdb"
        cn.Open()

        Dim rs As ADODB.Recordset = New ADODB.Recordset
        rs.ActiveConnection = cn
        rs.CursorLocation = 3
        rs.LockType = 3
        rs.let_Source("Select * From Products")
        rs.Open()

        Dim Da As New System.Data.OleDb.OleDbDataAdapter
        Dim dt As New System.Data.DataTable
        Da.Fill(dt, rs)

        populate_MSFlexgrid_Using_A_DataTable(dt, AxMSFlexGrid1,
"Multi Line Horizontal")

    End Sub

    Private Sub Button3_Click(sender As System.Object, e As
System.EventArgs) Handles Button3.Click

        Dim cn As ADODB.Connection = New ADODB.Connection
        cn.ConnectionString =
"Provider=Microsoft.Jet.OleDb.4.0;Data Source=C:\Program Files
(x86)\Microsoft Visual Studio\VB98\NWind.mdb"
        cn.Open()

        Dim rs As ADODB.Recordset = New ADODB.Recordset
        rs.ActiveConnection = cn
        rs.CursorLocation = 3
        rs.LockType = 3
        rs.let_Source("Select * From Products")
        rs.Open()

        Dim Da As New System.Data.OleDb.OleDbDataAdapter
        Dim dt As New System.Data.DataTable
        Da.Fill(dt, rs)

        populate_MSFlexgrid_Using_A_DataTable(dt, AxMSFlexGrid1,
"Single Line Vertical")

    End Sub
```

```vb
    Private Sub Button4_Click(sender As System.Object, e As
System.EventArgs) Handles Button4.Click


        Dim cn As ADODB.Connection = New ADODB.Connection
        cn.ConnectionString =
"Provider=Microsoft.Jet.OleDb.4.0;Data Source=C:\Program Files
(x86)\Microsoft Visual Studio\VB98\NWind.mdb"
        cn.Open()

        Dim rs As ADODB.Recordset = New ADODB.Recordset
        rs.ActiveConnection = cn
        rs.CursorLocation = 3
        rs.LockType = 3
        rs.let_Source("Select * From Products")
        rs.Open()

        Dim Da As New System.Data.OleDb.OleDbDataAdapter
        Dim dt As New System.Data.DataTable
        Da.Fill(dt, rs)

        populate_MSFlexgrid_Using_A_DataTable(dt, AxMSFlexGrid1,
"Multi Line Vertical")

    End Sub
```

The code that receives the request:

```vb
    Public Sub populate_MSFlexgrid_Using_A_DataTable(ByVal dt As
System.Data.DataTable, ByVal MSFlexgrid1 As
AxMSFlexGridLib.AxMSFlexGrid, ByVal Orientation As String)

        Dim x As Integer = 0
        Dim y As Integer = 0

        Select Case Orientation

            Case "Single Line Horizontal"

                MSFlexgrid1.Rows = 2
                MSFlexgrid1.Cols = dt.Columns.Count + 1

                For x = 0 To dt.Columns.Count - 1
```

```vbnet
                    MSFlexgrid1.set_TextMatrix(0, x + 1,
dt.Columns(x).Caption)
                Next

                Dim dr As System.Data.DataRow = dt.Rows(0)
                For x = 0 To dt.Columns.Count - 1
                    Try
                        MSFlexgrid1.set_TextMatrix(1, x + 1,
dr.Item(dt.Columns(x).Caption))
                    Catch ex As Exception
                        MSFlexgrid1.set_TextMatrix(1, x + 1, "")
                    End Try
                Next

            Case "Multi Line Horizontal"


                MSFlexgrid1.Rows = dt.Rows.Count + 1
                MSFlexgrid1.Cols = dt.Columns.Count + 1

                For x = 0 To dt.Columns.Count - 1
                    MSFlexgrid1.set_TextMatrix(0, x + 1,
dt.Columns(x).Caption)
                Next


                For y = 0 To dt.Rows.Count - 1
                    For x = 0 To dt.Columns.Count - 1
                        Try
                            MSFlexgrid1.set_TextMatrix(y + 1, x +
1, dt.Rows(y).Item(dt.Columns(x).Caption))
                        Catch ex As Exception
                            MSFlexgrid1.set_TextMatrix(y + 1, x +
1, "")
                        End Try
                    Next

                Next

            Case "Single Line Vertical"


                MSFlexgrid1.Cols = 2
                MSFlexgrid1.Rows = dt.Columns.Count + 2
```

```vbnet
                For x = 0 To dt.Columns.Count - 1
                    MSFlexgrid1.set_TextMatrix(x + 1, 0,
dt.Columns(x).Caption)
                Next

                Dim dr As System.Data.DataRow = dt.Rows(0)
                For x = 0 To dt.Columns.Count - 1
                    Try
                        MSFlexgrid1.set_TextMatrix(x + 1, 1,
dr.Item(dt.Columns(x).Caption))
                    Catch ex As Exception
                        MSFlexgrid1.set_TextMatrix(x + 1, 1, "")
                    End Try
                Next


            Case "Multi Line Vertical"

                MSFlexgrid1.set_TextMatrix(0, 1, "Property Name")

                MSFlexgrid1.Cols = dt.Rows.Count + 1
                MSFlexgrid1.Rows = dt.Columns.Count + 1


                For y = 0 To dt.Rows.Count - 1
                    MSFlexgrid1.set_TextMatrix(0, y + 1, "Row" &
y)
                Next

                For x = 0 To dt.Columns.Count - 1
                    MSFlexgrid1.set_TextMatrix(x + 1, 0,
dt.Columns(x).Caption)
                    For y = 0 To dt.Rows.Count - 1
                        Try
                            MSFlexgrid1.set_TextMatrix(x + 1, y +
1, dt.Rows(y).Item(dt.Columns(x).Caption))
                        Catch ex As Exception
                            MSFlexgrid1.set_TextMatrix(x + 1, y +
1, "")
                        End Try
                    Next

                Next

        End Select
```

```
        End Sub


    MSFlexgrid and DataView

The code that makes the request:

    Private Sub Button1_Click(sender As System.Object, e As
System.EventArgs) Handles Button1.Click

        Dim cn As ADODB.Connection = New ADODB.Connection
        cn.ConnectionString =
"Provider=Microsoft.Jet.OleDb.4.0;Data Source=C:\Program Files
(x86)\Microsoft Visual Studio\VB98\NWind.mdb"
        cn.Open()

        Dim rs As ADODB.Recordset = New ADODB.Recordset
        rs.ActiveConnection = cn
        rs.CursorLocation = 3
        rs.LockType = 3
        rs.let_Source("Select * From Products")
        rs.Open()

        Dim Da As New System.Data.OleDb.OleDbDataAdapter
        Dim dt As New System.Data.DataTable
        Da.Fill(dt, rs)

        populate_MSFlexgrid_Using_A_DataView(dt.DefaultView,
AxMSFlexGrid1, "Single Line Horizontal")

    End Sub

    Private Sub Button2_Click(sender As System.Object, e As
System.EventArgs) Handles Button2.Click

        Dim cn As ADODB.Connection = New ADODB.Connection
        cn.ConnectionString =
"Provider=Microsoft.Jet.OleDb.4.0;Data Source=C:\Program Files
(x86)\Microsoft Visual Studio\VB98\NWind.mdb"
        cn.Open()

        Dim rs As ADODB.Recordset = New ADODB.Recordset
```

```vb
        rs.ActiveConnection = cn
        rs.CursorLocation = 3
        rs.LockType = 3
        rs.let_Source("Select * From Products")
        rs.Open()

        Dim Da As New System.Data.OleDb.OleDbDataAdapter
        Dim dt As New System.Data.DataTable
        Da.Fill(dt, rs)

        populate_MSFlexgrid_Using_A_DataView(dt.DefaultView,
AxMSFlexGrid1, "Multi Line Horizontal")

    End Sub

    Private Sub Button3_Click(sender As System.Object, e As
System.EventArgs) Handles Button3.Click

        Dim cn As ADODB.Connection = New ADODB.Connection
        cn.ConnectionString =
"Provider=Microsoft.Jet.OleDb.4.0;Data Source=C:\Program Files
(x86)\Microsoft Visual Studio\VB98\NWind.mdb"
        cn.Open()

        Dim rs As ADODB.Recordset = New ADODB.Recordset
        rs.ActiveConnection = cn
        rs.CursorLocation = 3
        rs.LockType = 3
        rs.let_Source("Select * From Products")
        rs.Open()

        Dim Da As New System.Data.OleDb.OleDbDataAdapter
        Dim dt As New System.Data.DataTable
        Da.Fill(dt, rs)

        populate_MSFlexgrid_Using_A_DataView(dt.DefaultView,
AxMSFlexGrid1, "Single Line Vertical")

    End Sub

    Private Sub Button4_Click(sender As System.Object, e As
System.EventArgs) Handles Button4.Click


        Dim cn As ADODB.Connection = New ADODB.Connection
```

```vb
        cn.ConnectionString =
"Provider=Microsoft.Jet.OleDb.4.0;Data Source=C:\Program Files
(x86)\Microsoft Visual Studio\VB98\NWind.mdb"
        cn.Open()

        Dim rs As ADODB.Recordset = New ADODB.Recordset
        rs.ActiveConnection = cn
        rs.CursorLocation = 3
        rs.LockType = 3
        rs.let_Source("Select * From Products")
        rs.Open()

        Dim Da As New System.Data.OleDb.OleDbDataAdapter
        Dim dt As New System.Data.DataTable
        Da.Fill(dt, rs)

        populate_MSFlexgrid_Using_A_DataView(dt.DefaultView,
AxMSFlexGrid1, "Multi Line Vertical")

    End Sub
```

The code that receives the request:

```vb
    Public Sub populate_MSFlexgrid_Using_A_DataView(ByVal dv As
System.Data.DataView, ByVal MSFlexgrid1 As
AxMSFlexGridLib.AxMSFlexGrid, ByVal Orientation As String)

        Dim x As Integer = 0
        Dim y As Integer = 0

        Select Case Orientation

            Case "Single Line Horizontal"

                MSFlexgrid1.Rows = 2
                MSFlexgrid1.Cols = dv.Table.Columns.Count + 1

                For x = 0 To dv.Table.Columns.Count - 1
                    MSFlexgrid1.set_TextMatrix(0, x + 1,
dv.Table.Columns(x).Caption)
```

```vb
                Next

                Dim dr As System.Data.DataRow = dv.Table.Rows(0)
                For x = 0 To dv.Table.Columns.Count - 1
                    Try
                        MSFlexgrid1.set_TextMatrix(1, x + 1,
dr.Item(dv.Table.Columns(x).Caption))
                    Catch ex As Exception
                        MSFlexgrid1.set_TextMatrix(1, x + 1, "")
                    End Try
                Next

            Case "Multi Line Horizontal"


                MSFlexgrid1.Rows = dv.Table.Rows.Count + 1
                MSFlexgrid1.Cols = dv.Table.Columns.Count + 1

                For x = 0 To dv.Table.Columns.Count - 1
                    MSFlexgrid1.set_TextMatrix(0, x + 1,
dv.Table.Columns(x).Caption)
                Next


                For y = 0 To dv.Table.Rows.Count - 1
                    For x = 0 To dv.Table.Columns.Count - 1
                        Try
                            MSFlexgrid1.set_TextMatrix(y + 1, x +
1, dv.Table.Rows(y).Item(dv.Table.Columns(x).Caption))
                        Catch ex As Exception
                            MSFlexgrid1.set_TextMatrix(y + 1, x +
1, "")
                        End Try
                    Next

                Next

            Case "Single Line Vertical"


                MSFlexgrid1.Cols = 2
                MSFlexgrid1.Rows = dv.Table.Columns.Count + 2

                For x = 0 To dv.Table.Columns.Count - 1
```

```vb
                    MSFlexgrid1.set_TextMatrix(x + 1, 0,
dv.Table.Columns(x).Caption)
                Next

                Dim dr As System.Data.DataRow = dv.Table.Rows(0)
                For x = 0 To dv.Table.Columns.Count - 1
                    Try
                        MSFlexgrid1.set_TextMatrix(x + 1, 1,
dr.Item(dv.Table.Columns(x).Caption))
                    Catch ex As Exception
                        MSFlexgrid1.set_TextMatrix(x + 1, 1, "")
                    End Try
                Next


            Case "Multi Line Vertical"

                MSFlexgrid1.set_TextMatrix(0, 1, "Property Name")

                MSFlexgrid1.Cols = dv.Table.Rows.Count + 1
                MSFlexgrid1.Rows = dv.Table.Columns.Count + 1


                For y = 0 To dv.Table.Rows.Count - 1
                    MSFlexgrid1.set_TextMatrix(0, y + 1, "Row" &
y)
                Next

                For x = 0 To dv.Table.Columns.Count - 1
                    MSFlexgrid1.set_TextMatrix(x + 1, 0,
dv.Table.Columns(x).Caption)
                    For y = 0 To dv.Table.Rows.Count - 1
                        Try
                            MSFlexgrid1.set_TextMatrix(x + 1, y +
1, dv.Table.Rows(y).Item(dv.Table.Columns(x).Caption))
                        Catch ex As Exception
                            MSFlexgrid1.set_TextMatrix(x + 1, y +
1, "")
                        End Try
                    Next

                Next

        End Select
    End Sub
```

OWC Spreadsheet Control

The code below will populate the OWC Spreadsheet Control:

Below is the code that makes the requests.

```
Dim xmldoc As New System.Xml.XmlDocument
    xmldoc.Load("C:\Products.xml")
    Dim nl As System.Xml.XmlNodeList =
xmldoc.GetElementsByTagName("Products")
    populate_Spreadsheet_Using_Element_XML(nl,
AxSpreadsheet1, "Single Line Horizontal")

    End Sub

    Private Sub Button2_Click(sender As System.Object, e As
System.EventArgs) Handles Button2.Click

        Dim xmldoc As New System.Xml.XmlDocument
        xmldoc.Load("C:\Products.xml")
        Dim nl As System.Xml.XmlNodeList =
xmldoc.GetElementsByTagName("Products")
        populate_Spreadsheet_Using_Element_XML(nl,
AxSpreadsheet1, "Multi Line Horizontal")

    End Sub

    Private Sub Button3_Click(sender As System.Object, e As
System.EventArgs) Handles Button3.Click
        Dim xmldoc As New System.Xml.XmlDocument
```

```vb
        xmldoc.Load("C:\Products.xml")
        Dim nl As System.Xml.XmlNodeList =
xmldoc.GetElementsByTagName("Products")
        populate_Spreadsheet_Using_Element_XML(nl,
AxSpreadsheet1, "Single Line Vertical")

    End Sub

    Private Sub Button4_Click(sender As System.Object, e As
System.EventArgs) Handles Button4.Click

        Dim xmldoc As New System.Xml.XmlDocument
        xmldoc.Load("C:\Products.xml")
        Dim nl As System.Xml.XmlNodeList =
xmldoc.GetElementsByTagName("Products")
        populate_Spreadsheet_Using_Element_XML(nl,
AxSpreadsheet1, "Multi Line Vertical")

    End Sub
```

Below is the code that receives the requests;

```vb
    Public Sub populate_Spreadsheet_Using_A_Recordset(ByVal rs As
Object, ByVal sp1 As
AxMicrosoft.Office.Interop.Owc11.AxSpreadsheet, ByVal Orientation
As String)

        Dim x As Integer = 0
        Dim y As Integer = 2

        sp1.ActiveSheet.Cells.ClearContents()

        Select Case Orientation

            Case "Single Line Horizontal"

                For x = 0 To rs.Fields.Count - 1
                    sp1.ActiveSheet.Cells(1, x + 1) =
rs.Fields(x).Name
                Next
                rs.MoveFirst()
                For x = 0 To rs.Fields.Count - 1
```

```vb
                    Try
                        sp1.ActiveSheet.Cells(y, x + 1) =
rs.Fields(x).Value
                    Catch ex As Exception
                        sp1.ActiveSheet.Cells(y, x + 1) = ""
                    End Try
                Next

            Case "Multi Line Horizontal"

                For x = 0 To rs.Fields.Count - 1
                    sp1.ActiveSheet.Cells(1, x + 1) =
rs.Fields(x).Name
                Next
                rs.MoveFirst()

                rs.MoveFirst()
                Do While rs.EOF = False
                    For x = 0 To rs.Fields.Count - 1
                        Try
                            sp1.ActiveSheet.Cells(y, x + 1) =
rs.Fields(x).Value
                        Catch ex As Exception
                            sp1.ActiveSheet.Cells(y, x + 1) = ""
                        End Try
                    Next
                    y = y + 1
                    rs.MoveNext()
                Loop

            Case "Single Line Vertical"

                sp1.ActiveSheet.Cells(1, 1) = "Property Name"
                sp1.ActiveSheet.Cells(1, 2) = "Property Value"


                For x = 0 To rs.Fields.Count - 1
                    sp1.ActiveSheet.Cells(x + 1, 1) =
rs.Fields(x).Name
                    Try
                        sp1.ActiveSheet.Cells(x + 1, y) =
rs.Fields(x).Value
                    Catch ex As Exception
                        sp1.ActiveSheet.Cells(x + 1, y) = ""
                    End Try
```

```
            Next

        Case "Multi Line Vertical"

            rs.MoveFirst()
            Do While rs.EOF = False
                For x = 0 To rs.Fields.Count - 1
                    sp1.ActiveSheet.Cells(x + 1, 1) =
rs.Fields(x).Name
                    Try
                        sp1.ActiveSheet.Cells(x + 1, y) =
rs.Fields(x).Value
                    Catch ex As Exception
                        sp1.ActiveSheet.Cells(x + 1, y) = ""
                    End Try
                Next
                y = y + 1
                rs.MoveNext()
            Loop

        End Select

    End Sub
```

Here is the Single line horizontal view:

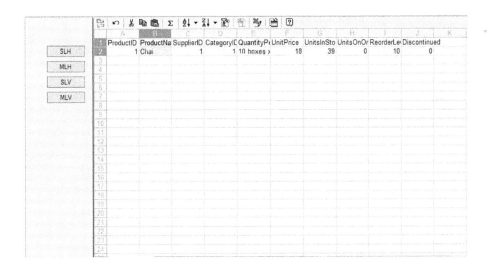

Here is the multi-line horizontal view:

ProductID	ProductName	SupplierID	CategoryID	QuantityPerUnit	UnitPrice	UnitsInStock	UnitsOnOrder	ReorderLevel	Discontinued
1	Chai	1	1	10 boxes x	18	39	0	10	0
2	Chang	1	1	24 - 12 oz	19	17	40	25	0
3	Aniseed S	1	2	12 - 550 m	10	13	70	25	0
4	Chef Antor	2	2	48 - 6 oz j	22	53	0	0	0
5	Chef Antor	2	2	36 boxes	21.35	0	0	0	1
6	Grandma's	3	2	12 - 8 oz j	25	120	0	25	0
7	Uncle Bob	3	7	12 - 1 lb pl	30	15	0	10	0
8	Northwood	3	2	12 - 12 oz	40	6	0	0	0
9	Mishi Kob	4	6	18 - 500 g	97	29	0	0	1
10	Ikura	4	8	12 - 200 m	31	31	0	0	0
11	Queso Cal	5	4	1 kg pkg.	21	22	30	30	0
12	Queso Ma	5	4	10 - 500 g	38	86	0	0	0
13	Konbu	6	8	2 kg box	6	24	0	5	0
14	Tofu	6	7	40 - 100 g	23.25	35	0	0	0
15	Genen Sho	6	2	24 - 250 m	15.5	39	0	5	0
16	Pavlova	7	3	32 - 500 g	17.45	29	0	10	0
17	Alice Mutt	7	6	20 - 1 kg ti	39	0	0	0	1
18	Carnarvon	7	8	16 kg pkg.	62.5	42	0	0	0
19	Teatime Cl	8	3	10 boxes x	9.2	25	0	5	0
20	Sir Rodney	8	3	30 gift box	81	40	0	0	0
21	Sir Rodney	8	3	24 pkgs. x	10	3	40	5	0
22	Gustaf's K	9	5	24 - 500 g	21	104	0	25	0
23	Tunnbröd	9	5	12 - 250 g	9	61	0	25	0

Here is the single line vertical view:

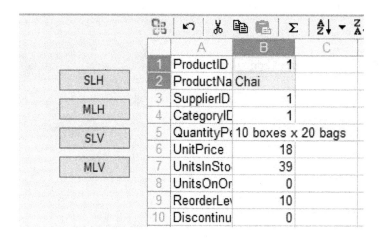

	A	B	C
1	ProductID	1	
2	ProductNa	Chai	
3	SupplierID	1	
4	CategoryID	1	
5	QuantityPe	10 boxes x 20 bags	
6	UnitPrice	18	
7	UnitsInSto	39	
8	UnitsOnOr	0	
9	ReorderLe	10	
10	Discontinu	0	

Here's the multi-line vertical view:

	A	B	C	D	E	F	G	H	I	J	K
1	ProductID	1	2	3	4	5	6	7	8	9	10
2	ProductNa	Chai	Chang	Aniseed S	Chef Antor	Chef Antor	Grandma's	Uncle Bob	Northwood	Mishi Kob	Ikura
3	SupplierID	1	1	1	2	2	3	3	3	4	4
4	CategoryID	1	1	2	2	2	2	7	2	6	8
5	QuantityPe	10 boxes x	24 - 12 oz	12 - 550 m	48 - 6 oz j	36 boxes	12 - 8 oz j	12 - 1 lb p	12 - 12 oz	18 - 500 g	12 - 200 m
6	UnitPrice	18	19	10	22	21.35	25	30	40	97	31
7	UnitsInSto	39	17	13	53	0	120	15	6	29	31
8	UnitsOnOr	0	40	70	0	0	0	0	0	0	0
9	ReorderLe	10	25	25	0	0	25	10	0	0	0
10	Discontinu	0	0	0	0	1	0	0	0	1	0

(Row buttons on left: SLH, MLH, SLV, MLV)

Spreadsheet and DataSet

The requesting code:

```
    Private Sub Button1_Click(sender As System.Object, e As
System.EventArgs) Handles Button1.Click

        Dim cn As ADODB.Connection = New ADODB.Connection
        cn.ConnectionString =
"Provider=Microsoft.Jet.OleDb.4.0;Data Source=C:\Program Files
(x86)\Microsoft Visual Studio\VB98\NWind.mdb"
        cn.Open()

        Dim rs As ADODB.Recordset = New ADODB.Recordset
        rs.ActiveConnection = cn
        rs.CursorLocation = 3
        rs.LockType = 3
        rs.let_Source("Select * From Products")
        rs.Open()

        Dim Da As New System.Data.OleDb.OleDbDataAdapter
        Dim ds As New System.Data.DataSet
        Da.Fill(ds, rs, "Products")

        populate_Spreadsheet_Using_A_DataSet(ds, AxSpreadsheet1,
"Single Line Horizontal")

    End Sub

    Private Sub Button2_Click(sender As System.Object, e As
System.EventArgs) Handles Button2.Click

        Dim cn As ADODB.Connection = New ADODB.Connection
```

```vb
        cn.ConnectionString =
"Provider=Microsoft.Jet.OleDb.4.0;Data Source=C:\Program Files
(x86)\Microsoft Visual Studio\VB98\NWind.mdb"
        cn.Open()

        Dim rs As ADODB.Recordset = New ADODB.Recordset
        rs.ActiveConnection = cn
        rs.CursorLocation = 3
        rs.LockType = 3
        rs.let_Source("Select * From Products")
        rs.Open()

        Dim Da As New System.Data.OleDb.OleDbDataAdapter
        Dim ds As New System.Data.DataSet
        Da.Fill(ds, rs, "Products")

        populate_Spreadsheet_Using_A_DataSet(ds, AxSpreadsheet1,
"Multi Line Horizontal")

    End Sub

    Private Sub Button3_Click(sender As System.Object, e As
System.EventArgs) Handles Button3.Click

        Dim cn As ADODB.Connection = New ADODB.Connection
        cn.ConnectionString =
"Provider=Microsoft.Jet.OleDb.4.0;Data Source=C:\Program Files
(x86)\Microsoft Visual Studio\VB98\NWind.mdb"
        cn.Open()

        Dim rs As ADODB.Recordset = New ADODB.Recordset
        rs.ActiveConnection = cn
        rs.CursorLocation = 3
        rs.LockType = 3
        rs.let_Source("Select * From Products")
        rs.Open()

        Dim Da As New System.Data.OleDb.OleDbDataAdapter
        Dim ds As New System.Data.DataSet
        Da.Fill(ds, rs, "Products")

        populate_Spreadsheet_Using_A_DataSet(ds, AxSpreadsheet1,
"Single Line Vertical")

    End Sub
```

```vb
    Private Sub Button4_Click(sender As System.Object, e As
System.EventArgs) Handles Button4.Click


        Dim cn As ADODB.Connection = New ADODB.Connection
        cn.ConnectionString =
"Provider=Microsoft.Jet.OleDb.4.0;Data Source=C:\Program Files
(x86)\Microsoft Visual Studio\VB98\NWind.mdb"
        cn.Open()

        Dim rs As ADODB.Recordset = New ADODB.Recordset
        rs.ActiveConnection = cn
        rs.CursorLocation = 3
        rs.LockType = 3
        rs.let_Source("Select * From Products")
        rs.Open()

        Dim Da As New System.Data.OleDb.OleDbDataAdapter
        Dim ds As New System.Data.DataSet
        Da.Fill(ds, rs, "Products")

        populate_Spreadsheet_Using_A_DataSet(ds, AxSpreadsheet1,
"Multi Line Vertical")

    End Sub
```

The receiving code:

```vb
    Public Sub populate_Spreadsheet_Using_A_DataSet(ByVal ds As
System.Data.DataSet, ByVal sp1 As
AxMicrosoft.Office.Interop.Owc11.AxSpreadsheet, ByVal Orientation
As String)

        Dim x As Integer = 0
        Dim y As Integer = 2

        sp1.ActiveSheet.Cells.ClearContents()

        Select Case Orientation

            Case "Single Line Horizontal"
```

```vbnet
                For x = 0 To ds.Tables(0).Columns.Count - 1
                    sp1.ActiveSheet.Cells(1, x + 1) =
ds.Tables(0).Columns(x).Caption
                Next
                Dim dr As System.Data.DataRow =
ds.Tables(0).Rows(0)
                For x = 0 To ds.Tables(0).Columns.Count - 1
                    Try
                        sp1.ActiveSheet.Cells(2, x + 1) =
dr.Item(ds.Tables(0).Columns(x).Caption)
                    Catch ex As Exception
                        sp1.ActiveSheet.Cells(2, x + 1) = ""
                    End Try
                Next

            Case "Multi Line Horizontal"

                For x = 0 To ds.Tables(0).Columns.Count - 1
                    sp1.ActiveSheet.Cells(1, x + 1) =
ds.Tables(0).Columns(x).Caption
                Next

                For y = 0 To ds.Tables(0).Rows.Count - 1
                    For x = 0 To ds.Tables(0).Columns.Count - 1
                        Try
                            sp1.ActiveSheet.Cells(y + 2, x + 1) =
ds.Tables(0).Rows(y).Item(ds.Tables(0).Columns(x).Caption)
                        Catch ex As Exception
                            sp1.ActiveSheet.Cells(y + 2, x + 1) =
""
                        End Try
                    Next
                Next


            Case "Single Line Vertical"

                sp1.ActiveSheet.Cells(1, 1) = "Property Name"
                sp1.ActiveSheet.Cells(1, 2) = "Property Value"


                For x = 0 To ds.Tables(0).Columns.Count - 1
                    sp1.ActiveSheet.Cells(x + 1, 1) =
ds.Tables(0).Columns(x).Caption
```

```
                Next

                    Dim dr As System.Data.DataRow =
ds.Tables(0).Rows(0)
                    For x = 0 To ds.Tables(0).Columns.Count - 1
                        Try
                            sp1.ActiveSheet.Cells(x + 1, 2) =
dr.Item(ds.Tables(0).Columns(x).Caption)
                        Catch ex As Exception
                            sp1.ActiveSheet.Cells(x + 1, 2) = ""
                        End Try
                    Next

            Case "Multi Line Vertical"

                    For x = 0 To ds.Tables(0).Columns.Count - 1
                        sp1.ActiveSheet.Cells(x + 1, 1) =
ds.Tables(0).Columns(x).Caption
                    Next

                    For y = 0 To ds.Tables(0).Rows.Count - 1
                        For x = 0 To ds.Tables(0).Columns.Count - 1
                            Try
                                sp1.ActiveSheet.Cells(x + 1, y + 2) =
ds.Tables(0).Rows(y).Item(ds.Tables(0).Columns(x).Caption)
                            Catch ex As Exception
                                sp1.ActiveSheet.Cells(x + 1, y + 2) =
""
                            End Try
                        Next
                    Next

        End Select

    End Sub
```

Spreadsheet and DataTable

Below is the requesting code:

```
    Private Sub Button1_Click(sender As System.Object, e As
System.EventArgs) Handles Button1.Click
```

```vb
        Dim cn As ADODB.Connection = New ADODB.Connection
        cn.ConnectionString =
"Provider=Microsoft.Jet.OleDb.4.0;Data Source=C:\Program Files
(x86)\Microsoft Visual Studio\VB98\NWind.mdb"
        cn.Open()

        Dim rs As ADODB.Recordset = New ADODB.Recordset
        rs.ActiveConnection = cn
        rs.CursorLocation = 3
        rs.LockType = 3
        rs.let_Source("Select * From Products")
        rs.Open()

        Dim Da As New System.Data.OleDb.OleDbDataAdapter
        Dim dt As New System.Data.DataTable
        Da.Fill(dt, rs)

        populate_Spreadsheet_Using_A_DataTable(dt,
AxSpreadsheet1, "Single Line Horizontal")

    End Sub

    Private Sub Button2_Click(sender As System.Object, e As
System.EventArgs) Handles Button2.Click

        Dim cn As ADODB.Connection = New ADODB.Connection
        cn.ConnectionString =
"Provider=Microsoft.Jet.OleDb.4.0;Data Source=C:\Program Files
(x86)\Microsoft Visual Studio\VB98\NWind.mdb"
        cn.Open()

        Dim rs As ADODB.Recordset = New ADODB.Recordset
        rs.ActiveConnection = cn
        rs.CursorLocation = 3
        rs.LockType = 3
        rs.let_Source("Select * From Products")
        rs.Open()

        Dim Da As New System.Data.OleDb.OleDbDataAdapter
        Dim dt As New System.Data.DataTable
        Da.Fill(dt, rs)

        populate_Spreadsheet_Using_A_DataTable(dt,
AxSpreadsheet1, "Multi Line Horizontal")
```

```vbnet
        End Sub

    Private Sub Button3_Click(sender As System.Object, e As
System.EventArgs) Handles Button3.Click

        Dim cn As ADODB.Connection = New ADODB.Connection
        cn.ConnectionString =
"Provider=Microsoft.Jet.OleDb.4.0;Data Source=C:\Program Files
(x86)\Microsoft Visual Studio\VB98\NWind.mdb"
        cn.Open()

        Dim rs As ADODB.Recordset = New ADODB.Recordset
        rs.ActiveConnection = cn
        rs.CursorLocation = 3
        rs.LockType = 3
        rs.let_Source("Select * From Products")
        rs.Open()

        Dim Da As New System.Data.OleDb.OleDbDataAdapter
        Dim dt As New System.Data.DataTable
        Da.Fill(dt, rs)

        populate_Spreadsheet_Using_A_DataTable(dt,
AxSpreadsheet1, "Single Line Vertical")

    End Sub

    Private Sub Button4_Click(sender As System.Object, e As
System.EventArgs) Handles Button4.Click


        Dim cn As ADODB.Connection = New ADODB.Connection
        cn.ConnectionString =
"Provider=Microsoft.Jet.OleDb.4.0;Data Source=C:\Program Files
(x86)\Microsoft Visual Studio\VB98\NWind.mdb"
        cn.Open()

        Dim rs As ADODB.Recordset = New ADODB.Recordset
        rs.ActiveConnection = cn
        rs.CursorLocation = 3
        rs.LockType = 3
        rs.let_Source("Select * From Products")
        rs.Open()

        Dim Da As New System.Data.OleDb.OleDbDataAdapter
```

```vb
        Dim dt As New System.Data.DataTable
        Da.Fill(dt, rs)

        populate_Spreadsheet_Using_A_DataTable(dt,
AxSpreadsheet1, "Multi Line Vertical")

    End Sub
```

Below is the receiving code:

```vb
    Public Sub populate_Spreadsheet_Using_A_DataTable(ByVal dt As
System.Data.DataTable, ByVal sp1 As
AxMicrosoft.Office.Interop.Owc11.AxSpreadsheet, ByVal Orientation
As String)

        Dim x As Integer = 0
        Dim y As Integer = 2

        sp1.ActiveSheet.Cells.ClearContents()

        Select Case Orientation

            Case "Single Line Horizontal"

                For x = 0 To dt.Columns.Count - 1
                    sp1.ActiveSheet.Cells(1, x + 1) =
dt.Columns(x).Caption
                Next
                Dim dr As System.Data.DataRow = dt.Rows(0)
                For x = 0 To dt.Columns.Count - 1
                    Try
                        sp1.ActiveSheet.Cells(2, x + 1) =
dr.Item(dt.Columns(x).Caption)
                    Catch ex As Exception
                        sp1.ActiveSheet.Cells(2, x + 1) = ""
                    End Try
                Next

            Case "Multi Line Horizontal"

                For x = 0 To dt.Columns.Count - 1
                    sp1.ActiveSheet.Cells(1, x + 1) =
dt.Columns(x).Caption
```

```vb
            Next

            For y = 0 To dt.Rows.Count - 1
                For x = 0 To dt.Columns.Count - 1
                    Try
                        sp1.ActiveSheet.Cells(y + 2, x + 1) =
dt.Rows(y).Item(dt.Columns(x).Caption)
                    Catch ex As Exception
                        sp1.ActiveSheet.Cells(y + 2, x + 1) =
""
                    End Try
                Next
            Next


        Case "Single Line Vertical"

            sp1.ActiveSheet.Cells(1, 1) = "Property Name"
            sp1.ActiveSheet.Cells(1, 2) = "Property Value"


            For x = 0 To dt.Columns.Count - 1
                sp1.ActiveSheet.Cells(x + 1, 1) =
dt.Columns(x).Caption
            Next

            Dim dr As System.Data.DataRow = dt.Rows(0)
            For x = 0 To dt.Columns.Count - 1
                Try
                    sp1.ActiveSheet.Cells(x + 1, 2) =
dr.Item(dt.Columns(x).Caption)
                Catch ex As Exception
                    sp1.ActiveSheet.Cells(x + 1, 2) = ""
                End Try
            Next

        Case "Multi Line Vertical"

            For x = 0 To dt.Columns.Count - 1
                sp1.ActiveSheet.Cells(x + 1, 1) =
dt.Columns(x).Caption
            Next

            For y = 0 To dt.Rows.Count - 1
                For x = 0 To dt.Columns.Count - 1
```

```
                        Try
                            sp1.ActiveSheet.Cells(x + 1, y + 2) =
dt.Rows(y).Item(dt.Columns(x).Caption)
                        Catch ex As Exception
                            sp1.ActiveSheet.Cells(x + 1, y + 2) =
""
                        End Try
                    Next
                Next

            End Select

        End Sub
```

Spreadsheet and DataView

Below is the requesting code:

```
    Private Sub Button1_Click(sender As System.Object, e As
System.EventArgs) Handles Button1.Click

        Dim cn As ADODB.Connection = New ADODB.Connection
        cn.ConnectionString =
"Provider=Microsoft.Jet.OleDb.4.0;Data Source=C:\Program Files
(x86)\Microsoft Visual Studio\VB98\NWind.mdb"
        cn.Open()

        Dim rs As ADODB.Recordset = New ADODB.Recordset
        rs.ActiveConnection = cn
        rs.CursorLocation = 3
        rs.LockType = 3
        rs.let_Source("Select * From Products")
        rs.Open()

        Dim Da As New System.Data.OleDb.OleDbDataAdapter
        Dim dt As New System.Data.DataTable
        Da.Fill(dt, rs)

        populate_Spreadsheet_Using_A_DataView(dt.DefaultView,
AxSpreadsheet1, "Single Line Horizontal")

    End Sub
```

```vb
    Private Sub Button2_Click(sender As System.Object, e As
System.EventArgs) Handles Button2.Click

        Dim cn As ADODB.Connection = New ADODB.Connection
        cn.ConnectionString =
"Provider=Microsoft.Jet.OleDb.4.0;Data Source=C:\Program Files
(x86)\Microsoft Visual Studio\VB98\NWind.mdb"
        cn.Open()

        Dim rs As ADODB.Recordset = New ADODB.Recordset
        rs.ActiveConnection = cn
        rs.CursorLocation = 3
        rs.LockType = 3
        rs.let_Source("Select * From Products")
        rs.Open()

        Dim Da As New System.Data.OleDb.OleDbDataAdapter
        Dim dt As New System.Data.DataTable
        Da.Fill(dt, rs)

        populate_Spreadsheet_Using_A_DataView(dt.DefaultView,
AxSpreadsheet1, "Multi Line Horizontal")

    End Sub

    Private Sub Button3_Click(sender As System.Object, e As
System.EventArgs) Handles Button3.Click

        Dim cn As ADODB.Connection = New ADODB.Connection
        cn.ConnectionString =
"Provider=Microsoft.Jet.OleDb.4.0;Data Source=C:\Program Files
(x86)\Microsoft Visual Studio\VB98\NWind.mdb"
        cn.Open()

        Dim rs As ADODB.Recordset = New ADODB.Recordset
        rs.ActiveConnection = cn
        rs.CursorLocation = 3
        rs.LockType = 3
        rs.let_Source("Select * From Products")
        rs.Open()

        Dim Da As New System.Data.OleDb.OleDbDataAdapter
        Dim dt As New System.Data.DataTable
        Da.Fill(dt, rs)
```

```
        populate_Spreadsheet_Using_A_DataView(dt.DefaultView,
AxSpreadsheet1, "Single Line Vertical")

    End Sub

    Private Sub Button4_Click(sender As System.Object, e As
System.EventArgs) Handles Button4.Click


        Dim cn As ADODB.Connection = New ADODB.Connection
        cn.ConnectionString =
"Provider=Microsoft.Jet.OleDb.4.0;Data Source=C:\Program Files
(x86)\Microsoft Visual Studio\VB98\NWind.mdb"
        cn.Open()

        Dim rs As ADODB.Recordset = New ADODB.Recordset
        rs.ActiveConnection = cn
        rs.CursorLocation = 3
        rs.LockType = 3
        rs.let_Source("Select * From Products")
        rs.Open()

        Dim Da As New System.Data.OleDb.OleDbDataAdapter
        Dim dt As New System.Data.DataTable
        Da.Fill(dt, rs)

        populate_Spreadsheet_Using_A_DataView(dt.DefaultView,
AxSpreadsheet1, "Multi Line Vertical")

    End Sub




Below is the receiving code:


    Public Sub populate_Spreadsheet_Using_A_DataView(ByVal dv As
System.Data.DataView, ByVal sp1 As
AxMicrosoft.Office.Interop.Owc11.AxSpreadsheet, ByVal Orientation
As String)

        Dim x As Integer = 0
        Dim y As Integer = 2
```

```vb
        sp1.ActiveSheet.Cells.ClearContents()

        Select Case Orientation

            Case "Single Line Horizontal"

                For x = 0 To dv.Table.Columns.Count - 1
                    sp1.ActiveSheet.Cells(1, x + 1) =
dv.Table.Columns(x).Caption
                Next
                Dim dr As System.Data.DataRow = dv.Table.Rows(0)
                For x = 0 To dv.Table.Columns.Count - 1
                    Try
                        sp1.ActiveSheet.Cells(2, x + 1) =
dr.Item(dv.Table.Columns(x).Caption)
                    Catch ex As Exception
                        sp1.ActiveSheet.Cells(2, x + 1) = ""
                    End Try
                Next

            Case "Multi Line Horizontal"

                For x = 0 To dv.Table.Columns.Count - 1
                    sp1.ActiveSheet.Cells(1, x + 1) =
dv.Table.Columns(x).Caption
                Next

                For y = 0 To dv.Table.Rows.Count - 1
                    For x = 0 To dv.Table.Columns.Count - 1
                        Try
                            sp1.ActiveSheet.Cells(y + 2, x + 1) =
dv.Table.Rows(y).Item(dv.Table.Columns(x).Caption)
                        Catch ex As Exception
                            sp1.ActiveSheet.Cells(y + 2, x + 1) =
""
                        End Try
                    Next
                Next

            Case "Single Line Vertical"

                sp1.ActiveSheet.Cells(1, 1) = "Property Name"
                sp1.ActiveSheet.Cells(1, 2) = "Property Value"
```

```vb
                For x = 0 To dv.Table.Columns.Count - 1
                    sp1.ActiveSheet.Cells(x + 1, 1) =
dv.Table.Columns(x).Caption
                Next

                Dim dr As System.Data.DataRow = dv.Table.Rows(0)
                For x = 0 To dv.Table.Columns.Count - 1
                    Try
                        sp1.ActiveSheet.Cells(x + 1, 2) =
dr.Item(dv.Table.Columns(x).Caption)
                    Catch ex As Exception
                        sp1.ActiveSheet.Cells(x + 1, 2) = ""
                    End Try
                Next

            Case "Multi Line Vertical"

                For x = 0 To dv.Table.Columns.Count - 1
                    sp1.ActiveSheet.Cells(x + 1, 1) =
dv.Table.Columns(x).Caption
                Next

                For y = 0 To dv.Table.Rows.Count - 1
                    For x = 0 To dv.Table.Columns.Count - 1
                        Try
                            sp1.ActiveSheet.Cells(x + 1, y + 2) =
dv.Table.Rows(y).Item(dv.Table.Columns(x).Caption)
                        Catch ex As Exception
                            sp1.ActiveSheet.Cells(x + 1, y + 2) =
""
                        End Try
                    Next
                Next

        End Select

    End Sub
```

Perhaps one of the easiest XML is Element XML

The pattern that needs to be created is the following:

```
<data>
    <rowname>
        <columnname>Columnvalue</columnname>
        <columnname>Columnvalue</columnname>
        <columnname>Columnvalue</columnname>
        <columnname>Columnvalue</columnname>
        <columnname>Columnvalue</columnname>
        <columnname>Columnvalue</columnname>
        <columnname>Columnvalue</columnname>
        <columnname>Columnvalue</columnname>
        <columnname>Columnvalue</columnname>
        <columnname>Columnvalue</columnname>
        <columnname>Columnvalue</columnname>
    </rowname>
</data>
```

```
Dim xmlDoc as new System.Xml.XmlDocument
xmldoc.Load("C:\Products.xml")
```

Dim NodeList as System.XML.XMLNodeList = xmlDoc.GetElementsByTagName("rowname")

Once we have a NodeList, we can then pass that over to our routine:

```
populate_Datagridview_Using_Element_XML(Nodelist, DataGridView1,
"Multi Line Horizontal")
```

```
Or:
```

```
populate_Listview_Using_Element_XML (Nodelist, ListView1, "Multi
Line Horizontal")
```

```
Or:
```

```
populate_MSFlexGrid_Using_Element_XML(Nodelist, AxMSFlexGrid1,
"Multi Line Horizontal")
```

```
Or:
```

```
populate_Spreadsheet_Using_Element_XML(Nodelist, AxSpreadsheet1,
"Multi Line Horizontal")
```

The code that receives the requests:

```vb
    Public Sub populate_Datagridview_Using_Element_XML(ByVal
Nodelist As System.Xml.XmlNodeList, ByVal Dg1 As DataGridView,
ByVal Orientation As String)

        Dim x As Integer = 0
        Dim y As Integer = 0

        Dg1.Rows.Clear()
        Dg1.Columns.Clear()

        Select Case Orientation

            Case "Single Line Horizontal"

                For x = 0 To Nodelist(0).ChildNodes.Count - 1

Dg1.Columns.Add(Nodelist(0).ChildNodes(x).Name,
Nodelist(0).ChildNodes(x).Name)
                Next
                Dg1.Rows.Add()
                For y = 0 To Nodelist.Count - 1
                    For x = 0 To Nodelist(y).ChildNodes.Count - 1
                        Try
                            Dg1.Rows(0).Cells(x).Value =
Nodelist(y).ChildNodes(x).InnerText
                        Catch cx As Exception
                            Dg1.Rows(0).Cells(x).Value = ""
                        End Try
                    Next
                    Exit For
                Next

            Case "Multi Line Horizontal"

                For x = 0 To Nodelist(0).ChildNodes.Count - 1

Dg1.Columns.Add(Nodelist(0).ChildNodes(x).Name,
Nodelist(0).ChildNodes(x).Name)
                Next
```

```vbnet
                For y = 0 To Nodelist.Count - 1
                    Dg1.Rows.Add()
                    For x = 0 To Nodelist(y).ChildNodes.Count - 1
                        Try
                            Dg1.Rows(y).Cells(x).Value =
Nodelist(y).ChildNodes(x).InnerText
                        Catch ex As Exception
                            Dg1.Rows(y).Cells(x).Value = ""
                        End Try
                    Next
                Next

            Case "Single Line Vertical"

                Dg1.Columns.Add("Property Name", "Property Name")
                Dg1.Columns.Add("Property Value", "Property
Value")
                For x = 0 To Nodelist(0).ChildNodes.Count - 1
                    Dg1.Rows.Add()
                    Dg1.Rows(x).Cells(0).Value =
Nodelist(0).ChildNodes(x).Name
                    Try
                        Dg1.Rows(x).Cells(1).Value =
Nodelist(0).ChildNodes(x).InnerText
                    Catch ex As Exception
                        Dg1.Rows(x).Cells(1).Value = ""
                    End Try
                Next

            Case "Multi Line Vertical"

                Dg1.Columns.Add(" Property Name", "Property
Name")

                For y = 0 To Nodelist.Count - 1
                    Dg1.Columns.Add("Row" & y, "Row" & y)
                Next

                For x = 0 To Nodelist(0).ChildNodes.Count - 1
                    Dg1.Rows.Add()
                    Dg1.Rows(x).Cells(0).Value =
Nodelist(0).ChildNodes(x).Name
                    For y = 0 To Nodelist.Count - 1
                        Try
```

```vb
                                    Dg1.Rows(x).Cells(y + 1).Value =
Nodelist(y).ChildNodes(x).InnerText
                        Catch ex As Exception
                            Dg1.Rows(x).Cells(y + 1).Value = ""
                        End Try
                Next
            Next

        End Select

    End Sub

    Public Sub populate_Listview_Using_Element_XML(ByVal Nodelist
As System.Xml.XmlNodeList, ByVal ListView1 As ListView, ByVal
Orientation As String)

        Dim x As Integer = 0
        Dim y As Integer = 0

        ListView1.Items.Clear()
        ListView1.Columns.Clear()

        Select Case Orientation

            Case "Single Line Horizontal"

                For x = 0 To Nodelist(0).ChildNodes.Count - 1

ListView1.Columns.Add(Nodelist(0).ChildNodes(x).Name)
                Next

                Dim li As ListViewItem
                For y = 0 To Nodelist.Count - 1
                    For x = 0 To Nodelist(y).ChildNodes.Count - 1
                        If x = 0 Then
                            Try
                                li =
ListView1.Items.Add(Nodelist(y).ChildNodes(x).InnerText)
                            Catch ex As Exception
                                li = ListView1.Items.Add("")
                            End Try

                        Else

                            Try
```

```vbnet
li.SubItems.Add(Nodelist(y).ChildNodes(x).InnerText)
                        Catch ex As Exception
                            li.SubItems.Add("")
                        End Try

                End If

            Next
            Exit For
        Next

    Case "Multi Line Horizontal"


        For x = 0 To Nodelist(0).ChildNodes.Count - 1

ListView1.Columns.Add(Nodelist(0).ChildNodes(x).Name)
        Next

        Dim li As ListViewItem
        For y = 0 To Nodelist.Count - 1
            For x = 0 To Nodelist(y).ChildNodes.Count - 1
                If x = 0 Then
                    Try
                        li =
ListView1.Items.Add(Nodelist(y).ChildNodes(x).InnerText)
                        Catch ex As Exception
                            li = ListView1.Items.Add("")
                        End Try

                Else

                    Try

li.SubItems.Add(Nodelist(y).ChildNodes(x).InnerText)
                        Catch ex As Exception
                            li.SubItems.Add("")
                        End Try

                End If

            Next

        Next
```

```vb
        Case "Single Line Vertical"

            ListView1.Columns.Add("Property Name")
            ListView1.Columns.Add("Property Value")

            Dim li As ListViewItem


            For x = 0 To Nodelist(y).ChildNodes.Count - 1
                li =
ListView1.Items.Add(Nodelist(0).ChildNodes(x).Name)
                Try

li.SubItems.Add(Nodelist(0).ChildNodes(x).InnerText)
                Catch ex As Exception
                    li.SubItems.Add("")
                End Try
            Next

        Case "Multi Line Vertical"

            ListView1.Columns.Add(" Property Name")
            Dim li As ListViewItem
            For y = 0 To Nodelist.Count - 1
                ListView1.Columns.Add("Row" & y)
            Next

            For x = 0 To Nodelist(0).ChildNodes.Count - 1
                li =
ListView1.Items.Add(Nodelist(0).ChildNodes(x).Name)
                For y = 0 To Nodelist.Count - 1
                    Try

li.SubItems.Add(Nodelist(y).ChildNodes(x).InnerText)
                    Catch ex As Exception
                        li.SubItems.Add("")
                    End Try
                Next
            Next

    End Select

End Sub
```

```vb
Public Sub populate_MSFlexgrid_Using_Element_XML(ByVal
Nodelist As System.Xml.XmlNodeList, ByVal MSFlexgrid1 As
AxMSFlexGridLib.AxMSFlexGrid, ByVal Orientation As String)

    Dim x As Integer = 0
    Dim y As Integer = 0

    MSFlexgrid1.Clear()

    Select Case Orientation

        Case "Single Line Horizontal"

            MSFlexgrid1.Rows = 2
            MSFlexgrid1.Cols = Nodelist(y).ChildNodes.Count +
1

            For x = 0 To Nodelist(0).ChildNodes.Count - 1
                MSFlexgrid1.set_TextMatrix(0, x + 1,
Nodelist(0).ChildNodes(x).Name)
            Next

            For x = 0 To Nodelist(0).ChildNodes.Count - 1
                Try
                    MSFlexgrid1.set_TextMatrix(1, x + 1,
Nodelist(0).ChildNodes(x).InnerText)
                Catch ex As Exception
                    MSFlexgrid1.set_TextMatrix(1, x + 1, "")
                End Try
            Next

        Case "Multi Line Horizontal"

            MSFlexgrid1.Rows = Nodelist.Count + 1
            MSFlexgrid1.Cols = Nodelist(0).ChildNodes.Count +
1

            For x = 0 To Nodelist(0).ChildNodes.Count - 1
                MSFlexgrid1.set_TextMatrix(0, x + 1,
Nodelist(0).ChildNodes(x).Name)
            Next

            For y = 0 To Nodelist.Count - 1
```

```
                    For x = 0 To Nodelist(y).ChildNodes.Count - 1
                        Try
                            MSFlexgrid1.set_TextMatrix(y + 1, x +
1, Nodelist(y).ChildNodes(x).InnerText)
                        Catch ex As Exception
                            MSFlexgrid1.set_TextMatrix(y + 1, x +
1, "")
                        End Try
                    Next
                Next


        Case "Single Line Vertical"


                MSFlexgrid1.Cols = 2
                MSFlexgrid1.Rows = Nodelist(y).ChildNodes.Count +
1

                For x = 0 To Nodelist(0).ChildNodes.Count - 1
                    MSFlexgrid1.set_TextMatrix(x + 1, 0,
Nodelist(0).ChildNodes(x).Name)
                Next

                For x = 0 To Nodelist(0).ChildNodes.Count - 1
                    Try
                        MSFlexgrid1.set_TextMatrix(x + 1, 1,
Nodelist(0).ChildNodes(x).InnerText)
                    Catch ex As Exception
                        MSFlexgrid1.set_TextMatrix(x + 1, 1, "")
                    End Try
                Next



        Case "Multi Line Vertical"

                MSFlexgrid1.set_TextMatrix(0, 0, "Property Name")

                MSFlexgrid1.Cols = Nodelist.Count + 1
                MSFlexgrid1.Rows = Nodelist(0).ChildNodes.Count +
1


                For y = 0 To Nodelist.Count - 1
```

```vb
                    MSFlexgrid1.set_TextMatrix(0, y + 1, "Row" &
y)
                Next

                For x = 0 To Nodelist(0).ChildNodes.Count - 1
                    MSFlexgrid1.set_TextMatrix(x + 1, 0,
Nodelist(0).ChildNodes(x).Name)
                    For y = 0 To Nodelist.Count - 1
                        Try
                            MSFlexgrid1.set_TextMatrix(x + 1, y +
1, Nodelist(y).ChildNodes(x).InnerText)
                        Catch ex As Exception
                            MSFlexgrid1.set_TextMatrix(x + 1, y +
1, "")
                        End Try
                    Next
                Next

        End Select

    End Sub


    Public Sub populate_Spreadsheet_Using_Element_XML(ByVal
Nodelist As System.Xml.XmlNodeList, ByVal sp1 As
AxMicrosoft.Office.Interop.Owc11.AxSpreadsheet, ByVal Orientation
As String)

        Dim x As Integer = 0
        Dim y As Integer = 2

        sp1.ActiveSheet.Cells.ClearContents()

        Select Case Orientation

            Case "Single Line Horizontal"

                For x = 0 To Nodelist(0).ChildNodes.Count - 1
                    sp1.ActiveSheet.Cells(1, x + 1) =
Nodelist(0).ChildNodes(x).Name
                Next

                For x = 0 To Nodelist(0).ChildNodes.Count - 1
                    Try
```

```vbnet
                        sp1.ActiveSheet.Cells(2, x + 1) =
Nodelist(0).ChildNodes(x).InnerText
                    Catch ex As Exception
                        sp1.ActiveSheet.Cells(2, x + 1) = ""
                    End Try
                Next


            Case "Multi Line Horizontal"


                For x = 0 To Nodelist(0).ChildNodes.Count - 1
                    sp1.ActiveSheet.Cells(1, x + 1) =
Nodelist(0).ChildNodes(x).Name
                Next

                For y = 0 To Nodelist.Count - 1
                    For x = 0 To Nodelist(0).ChildNodes.Count - 1
                        Try
                            sp1.ActiveSheet.Cells(y + 2, x + 1) =
Nodelist(y).ChildNodes(x).InnerText
                        Catch ex As Exception
                            sp1.ActiveSheet.Cells(y + 2, x + 1) =
""
                        End Try
                    Next

                Next


            Case "Single Line Vertical"


                For x = 0 To Nodelist(0).ChildNodes.Count - 1
                    sp1.ActiveSheet.Cells(x + 1, 1) =
Nodelist(y).ChildNodes(x).Name

                    Try
                        sp1.ActiveSheet.Cells(x + 1, 2) =
Nodelist(0).ChildNodes(x).InnerText
                    Catch ex As Exception
                        sp1.ActiveSheet.Cells(x + 1, 2) = ""
                    End Try
                Next
```

```vbnet
                Case "Multi Line Vertical"


                    For x = 0 To Nodelist(0).ChildNodes.Count - 1
                        sp1.ActiveSheet.Cells(x + 1, 1) =
Nodelist(0).ChildNodes(x).Name
                        For y = 0 To Nodelist.Count - 1
                            Try
                                sp1.ActiveSheet.Cells(x + 1, y + 2) =
Nodelist(y).ChildNodes(x).InnerText
                            Catch ex As Exception
                                sp1.ActiveSheet.Cells(x + 1, y + 2) =
""

                            End Try
                        Next
                    Next

            End Select

        End Sub
```

Working with Schema XML and MSPERSIST

When you open a recordset, you have the option to save the Recordset in two formats:

Microsoft Advanced Data TableGram format which = 0
Extensible Markup Language (XML) format which = 1

While Microsoft claims that MSPersist can read both, I use the Extensible Markup Language (XML) format to create what I call Schema XML. And again, since we have already covered Recordsets, All you have to do is plug in the code you want to use that creates a Recordset and then call the DataGridView, Listview, MSFlexgrid, or Spreadsheet routine to produce the type of orientation you want to see.

Using xml to render the information is a different story. The requesting code needs to be called this way:

Dim xmlDoc as new System.Xml.XmlDocument
xmldoc.Load("C:\ProductsSchema.xml")
Dim   NodeList   as   System.XML.XMLNodeList   =
xmlDoc.GetElementsByTagName("z:row")
Once we have a NodeList, we can then pass that over to our routine:

```
populate_Datagridview_Using_MSPERSIST(Nodelist, DataGridView1,
"Multi Line Horizontal")
```

Or:

```
populate_Listview_Using_MSPERSIST(Nodelist, ListView1, "Multi
Line Horizontal")
```

Or:

```
populate_MSFlexGrid_Using_MSPERSIST(Nodelist, AxMSFlexGrid1,
"Multi Line Horizontal")
```

Or:

```
populate_Spreadsheet_Using_MSPERSIST(Nodelist, AxSpreadsheet1,
"Multi Line Horizontal")
```

The code below accept the above calls. Also, notice the code is working with attributes instead of ChildNodes. That's because each row is the collection of columns or of fields on a single line.

```
    Public Sub populate_Datagridview_Using_MSPERSIST(ByVal
Nodelist As System.Xml.XmlNodeList, ByVal Dg1 As DataGridView,
ByVal Orientation As String)

        Dim x As Integer = 0
        Dim y As Integer = 0

        Dg1.Rows.Clear()
        Dg1.Columns.Clear()

        Select Case Orientation

            Case "Single Line Horizontal"

                For x = 0 To Nodelist(0).Attributes.Count - 1

Dg1.Columns.Add(Nodelist(0).Attributes(x).Name,
Nodelist(0).Attributes(x).Name)
                Next
                Dg1.Rows.Add()
                For y = 0 To Nodelist.Count - 1
                    For x = 0 To Nodelist(y).Attributes.Count - 1
```

```vbnet
                        Try
                            Dg1.Rows(0).Cells(x).Value =
Nodelist(y).Attributes(x).Value
                        Catch ex As Exception
                            Dg1.Rows(0).Cells(x).Value = ""
                        End Try
                    Next
                    Exit For
                Next

            Case "Multi Line Horizontal"

                For x = 0 To Nodelist(0).Attributes.Count - 1

Dg1.Columns.Add(Nodelist(0).Attributes(x).Name,
Nodelist(0).Attributes(x).Name)
                    Next

                For y = 0 To Nodelist.Count - 1
                    Dg1.Rows.Add()
                    For x = 0 To Nodelist(y).Attributes.Count - 1
                        Try
                            Dg1.Rows(y).Cells(x).Value =
Nodelist(y).Attributes(x).Value
                        Catch ex As Exception
                            Dg1.Rows(y).Cells(x).Value = ""
                        End Try
                    Next
                Next

            Case "Single Line Vertical"

                Dg1.Columns.Add("Property Name", "Property Name")
                Dg1.Columns.Add("Property Value", "Property
Value")
                For x = 0 To Nodelist(0).Attributes.Count - 1
                    Dg1.Rows.Add()
                    Dg1.Rows(x).Cells(0).Value =
Nodelist(0).Attributes(x).Name
                    Try
                        Dg1.Rows(x).Cells(1).Value =
Nodelist(0).Attributes(x).Value
                    Catch ex As Exception
                        Dg1.Rows(x).Cells(1).Value = ""
                    End Try
```

```vb
            Next

        Case "Multi Line Vertical"

            Dg1.Columns.Add(" Property Name", "Property
Name")

            For y = 0 To Nodelist.Count - 1
                Dg1.Columns.Add("Row" & y, "Row" & y)
            Next

            For x = 0 To Nodelist(0).Attributes.Count - 1
                Dg1.Rows.Add()
                Dg1.Rows(x).Cells(0).Value =
Nodelist(0).Attributes(x).Name
                For y = 0 To Nodelist.Count - 1
                    Try
                        Dg1.Rows(x).Cells(y + 1).Value =
Nodelist(y).Attributes(x).Value
                    Catch ex As Exception
                        Dg1.Rows(x).Cells(y + 1).Value = ""
                    End Try
                Next
            Next

    End Select

End Sub

Public Sub populate_Listview_Using_MSPERSIST(ByVal Nodelist
As System.Xml.XmlNodeList, ByVal ListView1 As ListView, ByVal
Orientation As String)

        Dim x As Integer = 0
        Dim y As Integer = 0

        ListView1.Items.Clear()
        ListView1.Columns.Clear()

        Select Case Orientation

            Case "Single Line Horizontal"

                For x = 0 To Nodelist(0).Attributes.Count - 1
```

```vbnet
ListView1.Columns.Add(Nodelist(0).Attributes(x).Name)
                Next

                Dim li As ListViewItem
                For y = 0 To Nodelist.Count - 1
                    For x = 0 To Nodelist(y).Attributes.Count - 1
                        If x = 0 Then
                            Try
                                li =
ListView1.Items.Add(Nodelist(y).Attributes(x).Value)
                            Catch ex As Exception
                                li = ListView1.Items.Add("")
                            End Try

                        Else

                            Try

li.SubItems.Add(Nodelist(y).Attributes(x).Value)
                            Catch ex As Exception
                                li.SubItems.Add("")
                            End Try

                        End If

                    Next
                    Exit For
                Next

            Case "Multi Line Horizontal"


                For x = 0 To Nodelist(0).Attributes.Count - 1

ListView1.Columns.Add(Nodelist(0).Attributes(x).Name)
                Next

                Dim li As ListViewItem
                For y = 0 To Nodelist.Count - 1
                    For x = 0 To Nodelist(y).Attributes.Count - 1
                        If x = 0 Then
                            Try
                                li =
ListView1.Items.Add(Nodelist(y).Attributes(x).Value)
```

```vbnet
                              Catch ex As Exception
                                  li = ListView1.Items.Add("")
                              End Try

                    Else

                        Try

li.SubItems.Add(Nodelist(y).Attributes(x).Value)
                              Catch ex As Exception
                                  li.SubItems.Add("")
                              End Try

                        End If

                Next

            Next

        Case "Single Line Vertical"

            ListView1.Columns.Add("Property Name")
            ListView1.Columns.Add("Property Value")

            Dim li As ListViewItem


            For x = 0 To Nodelist(y).Attributes.Count - 1
                li =
ListView1.Items.Add(Nodelist(0).Attributes(x).Name)
                Try

li.SubItems.Add(Nodelist(0).Attributes(x).Value)
                Catch ex As Exception
                    li.SubItems.Add("")
                End Try
            Next

        Case "Multi Line Vertical"

            ListView1.Columns.Add(" Property Name")
            Dim li As ListViewItem
            For y = 0 To Nodelist.Count - 1
                ListView1.Columns.Add("Row" & y)
            Next
```

```vb
                For x = 0 To Nodelist(0).Attributes.Count - 1
                    li =
ListView1.Items.Add(Nodelist(0).Attributes(x).Name)
                    For y = 0 To Nodelist.Count - 1
                        Try

li.SubItems.Add(Nodelist(y).Attributes(x).Value)
                        Catch ex As Exception
                            li.SubItems.Add("")
                        End Try
                    Next
                Next

        End Select

    End Sub


    Public Sub populate_MSFlexgrid_Using_MSPERSIST(ByVal Nodelist
As System.Xml.XmlNodeList, ByVal MSFlexgrid1 As
AxMSFlexGridLib.AxMSFlexGrid, ByVal Orientation As String)

        Dim x As Integer = 0
        Dim y As Integer = 0

        MSFlexgrid1.Clear()

        Select Case Orientation

            Case "Single Line Horizontal"

                MSFlexgrid1.Rows = 2
                MSFlexgrid1.Cols = Nodelist(y).Attributes.Count +
1

                For x = 0 To Nodelist(0).Attributes.Count - 1
                    MSFlexgrid1.set_TextMatrix(0, x + 1,
Nodelist(0).Attributes(x).Name)
                Next

                For x = 0 To Nodelist(0).Attributes.Count - 1
                    Try
                        MSFlexgrid1.set_TextMatrix(1, x + 1,
Nodelist(0).Attributes(x).Value)
```

```vb
            Catch ex As Exception
                MSFlexgrid1.set_TextMatrix(1, x + 1, "")
            End Try
        Next

    Case "Multi Line Horizontal"


        MSFlexgrid1.Rows = Nodelist.Count + 1
        MSFlexgrid1.Cols = Nodelist(0).Attributes.Count +
1


        For x = 0 To Nodelist(0).Attributes.Count - 1
            MSFlexgrid1.set_TextMatrix(0, x + 1,
Nodelist(0).Attributes(x).Name)
        Next

        For y = 0 To Nodelist.Count - 1
            For x = 0 To Nodelist(y).Attributes.Count - 1
                Try
                    MSFlexgrid1.set_TextMatrix(y + 1, x +
1, Nodelist(y).Attributes(x).Value)
                Catch ex As Exception
                    MSFlexgrid1.set_TextMatrix(y + 1, x +
1, "")
                End Try
            Next
        Next

    Case "Single Line Vertical"


        MSFlexgrid1.Cols = 2
        MSFlexgrid1.Rows = Nodelist(y).Attributes.Count +
1


        For x = 0 To Nodelist(0).Attributes.Count - 1
            MSFlexgrid1.set_TextMatrix(x + 1, 0,
Nodelist(0).Attributes(x).Name)
        Next

        For x = 0 To Nodelist(0).Attributes.Count - 1
            Try
                MSFlexgrid1.set_TextMatrix(x + 1, 1,
Nodelist(0).Attributes(x).Value)
```

```vbnet
                Catch ex As Exception
                    MSFlexgrid1.set_TextMatrix(x + 1, 1, "")
                End Try
            Next


        Case "Multi Line Vertical"

            MSFlexgrid1.set_TextMatrix(0, 0, "Property Name")

            MSFlexgrid1.Cols = Nodelist.Count + 1
            MSFlexgrid1.Rows = Nodelist(0).Attributes.Count +
1


            For y = 0 To Nodelist.Count - 1
                MSFlexgrid1.set_TextMatrix(0, y + 1, "Row" &
y)
            Next

            For x = 0 To Nodelist(0).Attributes.Count - 1
                MSFlexgrid1.set_TextMatrix(x + 1, 0,
Nodelist(0).Attributes(x).Name)
                For y = 0 To Nodelist.Count - 1
                    Try
                        MSFlexgrid1.set_TextMatrix(x + 1, y +
1, Nodelist(y).Attributes(x).Value)
                    Catch ex As Exception
                        MSFlexgrid1.set_TextMatrix(x + 1, y +
1, "")
                    End Try
                Next
            Next

    End Select

  End Sub


    Public Sub populate_Spreadsheet_Using_MSPERSIST(ByVal
Nodelist As System.Xml.XmlNodeList, ByVal sp1 As
AxMicrosoft.Office.Interop.Owc11.AxSpreadsheet, ByVal Orientation
As String)
```

```vbnet
        Dim x As Integer = 0
        Dim y As Integer = 2

        sp1.ActiveSheet.Cells.ClearContents()

        Select Case Orientation

            Case "Single Line Horizontal"

                For x = 0 To Nodelist(0).Attributes.Count - 1
                    sp1.ActiveSheet.Cells(1, x + 1) =
Nodelist(0).Attributes(x).Name
                Next

                For x = 0 To Nodelist(0).Attributes.Count - 1
                    Try
                        sp1.ActiveSheet.Cells(2, x + 1) =
Nodelist(0).Attributes(x).Value
                    Catch ex As Exception
                        sp1.ActiveSheet.Cells(2, x + 1) = ""
                    End Try
                Next


            Case "Multi Line Horizontal"

                For x = 0 To Nodelist(0).Attributes.Count - 1
                    sp1.ActiveSheet.Cells(1, x + 1) =
Nodelist(0).Attributes(x).Name
                Next

                For y = 0 To Nodelist.Count - 1
                    For x = 0 To Nodelist(0).Attributes.Count - 1
                        Try
                            sp1.ActiveSheet.Cells(y + 2, x + 1) =
Nodelist(y).Attributes(x).Value
                        Catch ex As Exception
                            sp1.ActiveSheet.Cells(y + 2, x + 1) =
""
                        End Try
                    Next

                Next
```

```vbnet
            Case "Single Line Vertical"


                For x = 0 To Nodelist(0).Attributes.Count - 1
                    sp1.ActiveSheet.Cells(x + 1, 1) =
Nodelist(y).Attributes(x).Name

                    Try
                        sp1.ActiveSheet.Cells(x + 1, 2) =
Nodelist(0).Attributes(x).Value
                    Catch ex As Exception
                        sp1.ActiveSheet.Cells(x + 1, 2) = ""
                    End Try
                Next



            Case "Multi Line Vertical"


                For x = 0 To Nodelist(0).Attributes.Count - 1
                    sp1.ActiveSheet.Cells(x + 1, 1) =
Nodelist(0).Attributes(x).Name
                    For y = 0 To Nodelist.Count - 1
                        Try
                            sp1.ActiveSheet.Cells(x + 1, y + 2) =
Nodelist(y).Attributes(x).Value
                        Catch ex As Exception
                            sp1.ActiveSheet.Cells(x + 1, y + 2) =
""
                        End Try
                    Next
                Next

        End Select

    End Sub
```

www.ingramcontent.com/pod-product-compliance
Lightning Source LLC
Chambersburg PA
CBHW070844070326
40690CB00009B/1690